Grading, Reporting, and Professional Judgment in Elementary Classrooms

Grading, Reporting, and Professional Judgment in Elementary Classrooms

Sandra Herbst
Anne Davies, Ph. D.

 connect2learning

Printed and bound in Canada by Hignell Book Printing.

18 17 16   6 5 4 3

Project Management: Judith Hall-Patch
Book Design: START Communications
Art and Design: Anne Davies, Cori Jones
Editor: Sheree North

Library and Archives Canada Cataloguing in Publication

Herbst, Sandra, 1970-, author
      Grading, Reporting, and Professional Judgment in Elementary
Classrooms / Sandra Herbst, Anne Davies, Ph.D..

Includes bibliographical references.
ISBN 978-1-928092-03-2 (paperback)

      1. Grading and marking (Students)--Canada. 2. Education, Elementary--Canada. I. Davies, Anne, 1955-, author II. Title.

LB3054.C3H47 2015   372.127,20971   C2015-906060-5

Additional copies of this book may be purchased from:

||ᚣ|| connect2learning

2449D Rosewall Crescent
Courtenay, BC V9N 8R9
CANADA
1-800-603-9888 (North America only)
1-250-703-2920
1-250-703-2921 (Fax)
books@connect2learning.com
www.connect2learning.com

Discounts available on bulk orders.

Contents

To Ann Sherman, for her unwavering support and advocacy of work
that makes a difference in students' lives.

Foreword

True professionals have autonomy. They are experts in their fields, and they are given latitude to make high-impact decisions. However (riffing on a theme from Stan Lee's *Spiderman*) with those strengths and freedoms comes responsibility.

In order to be useful, a teacher's assessment must create accurate reports of student progress, and they must be helpful to the feedback/instruction dynamic. This is not just a nice thing to do; it's a moral obligation. Seriously, the teacher who does not understand and use assessment effectively is committing educational malpractice. Parents do not want their child in that individual's classroom; there's too much at stake.

Sound assessment practices are not left to chance, as they permeate almost everything that happens in a classroom. While assessing the capacity to analyze literary devices in a novel, for example, we find that our student, Lamar, can't read independently at grade level – but we're using grade-level text to teach a concept. In response to this knowledge, we record the text aloud with proper vocal inflections that emphasize comprehension on an audio file, and we send it to Lamar. For struggling students, reading comprehension is much higher when text is read aloud by someone who understands it than when they themselves read the same text silently. After listening to the audio file, Lamar is able to make intellectually agile analyses of the text as easily as his independently reading classmates can. We report his high mark for analyzing literary devices in a novel: a 4.0. The earlier reading assessment informed our instructional response, and Lamar is able to thrive. We'll teach him to read at grade level eventually, but for this standard, his assessment report is accurate, and he achieves.

We shouldn't feel threatened when asked by an administrator to demonstrate how assessment informs our instructional decisions or how our grades are accurate reports of student progress. These are as natural as breathing to assessment-savvy practitioners. We don't teach in the dark, indifferent to the eager minds before us or the requirement that we are accurate in our reporting. Fear and indifference *are* what happen, however, if we don't have expertise and the tools that come with it.

Thank goodness for Sandra Herbst and Anne Davies who share the needed tools and insights for assessment and reporting as they do in *Grading, Reporting, and Professional Judgment in Elementary Classrooms*. With the assistance of their practicality, inspiration, and extended research, we zoom to a much higher level of expertise and effectiveness than we would achieve on our own or with other books about assessment. This book provides a clear vision of not only what to do, but how to do it, for new teachers seeking guidance and for seasoned veterans seeking fortitude and innovation to breathe new life into practices grown complacent or cynical. In short, the book has two gifts: a professional salve for the blistering wounds of the assessment/reporting juggernaut and a refreshing energizer for assessment/reporting fatigue, all wrapped in attentive professionalism.

Herbst and Davies know their stuff. They have decades of experience researching and implementing these ideas, as well as experience coaching teachers as they use them in their own classrooms. They have encountered every, "Yeah, but…" question and responded thoughtfully to each one, helping skeptics find the value in these practices. It's worth the price of the book just to have the, "How Do We Respond to This Pushback?" section alone. I've seen the positive results that come from reading the high-school version of this book, and I'm deeply grateful for this one, their version for primary and elementary teachers.

As undergraduates, so many of us took assessment courses in schools of teacher education that were mostly overviews of the history of testing, a few segments on validity, reliability, correlation, causation, qualitative versus quantitative data, and maybe something about why the standard deviation has merit. We may have learned about various instruments commonly used in schools, but our nervous, neophyte selves were secretly screaming:

> *How can I be held responsible for a student's whole future to be built or destroyed purely on my personal opinion and the one score I record at the top of a project? How do I design quizzes, tests, and prompts? How do I connect the dots between my assessments and my instructional response to students? How do I report student progress ethically and accurately? How do I know what a 4.0 performance is, and what are the lines of demarcation among all the rubrics scores in everything I teach? How do I know if my evaluative criteria are legitimate? Can I use homework and quizzes in the final grade report? What about reassessing for full credit, dealing with late work, or zeroes on the 100-point scale? And how do I keep up with all the record-keeping and defend my policies when parents or students complain?*

It's fine to tell us about the larger picture of education measurements and how we got here, but what we really need are the tools to navigate assessment's high-stakes waters. Honestly, I wish I had had the Herbst and Davies publications when I was an undergrad.

In my experience, teachers (including myself, earlier in my career) are poor self-assessors regarding assessment and reporting practices. They can define many of the "buzz" words in assessment and they claim that they employ best practices, but when asked to manifest all that wisdom in response to real classroom assessment challenges, they fall short. Many school divisions define letter grades for teachers, but when it comes to grading individual student assessments, most teachers fall back on their own emotional baggage for what they think constitutes performance for each letter grade, regardless of what the school division has declared. They also succumb to relativism when assessing, marking some students' performances with higher scores because "Henry worked so hard and had to overcome so much," or because "Kiki's was the first paper that showed promise after seven in a row that lacked anything substantive."

Teachers often say their grades are accurate reports of student learning, but they raise or lower grades based on what they think will motivate students, not based on the actual criteria of the evidence sought. They define basic concepts they have to teach with colleagues teaching the same subject and assert this as proof they have calibrated the evidence of the standards they're seeking – but they really didn't move beyond just the definition of terms. Their assessments are little more than proof of parroting. They never discussed what it means to be intellectually agile, to demonstrate mental dexterity or skill versatility with the concepts being taught, and their grades vary widely in meaning as a result. It's not urban legend; it's true: A student gets a "B" for a specific amount of learning in one class, yet that same amount of learning in another teacher's class in the same school and subject would yield an "A" or a "C."

Do consistency and honesty matter? Do assessment and grading integrity matter? Yes! Our whole enterprise is a sham without all four. Parents and communities are counting on us to get these right. They need to trust that what we assess is worthwhile, and what we report is true.

Kudos to Herbst and Davies for understanding this inconsistency between what teachers say they know and what they actually do. I don't blame teachers for falling into these misunderstandings though, and I bet Herbst and Davies don't either. We've all been there and made the same mistakes. We've evolved, however, as has the teaching profession, and today we have clear steps in this book on how to avoid these mistakes and do right by our students.

One of the coolest elements in Herbst and Davies' approach is to put students in the driver seat of their own assessment. Hattie, Marzano, Stiggins, Black, Wiliam, Cooper, and many more advocate for students to self-monitor where they are in relation to a learning target. This is more than an academic exercise; it's a life skill. Herbst and Davies provide very clear strategies on how to equip students to analyze and reflect upon their own work, and to adjust the next steps in their own learning as a result. Students thereby become active creators in their schooling instead of passive consumers. This is an amazing shift in thinking for many teachers, but it reflects the modern classroom beautifully. When students can articulate their learning goals and where they are in relation to those goals, they achieve their goals dramatically more often.

Of particular interest here, too, is the effect on student self-agency and resilience. The strategies that get students engaged in their own assessment presented here are many of the same ones used to cultivate the growth mindset popularized by Dr. Carol Dweck. As Dr. Dweck often emphasizes, do we teach students to come across as smart at all costs, or do we teach them to learn at all costs? Do we ask how many got a particular problem correct, or do we ask who had an interesting mistake and insight from its resolution to share? It's amazing how many parallels there are between the concepts in *Grading, Reporting, and Professional Judgment in Elementary Classrooms* and what we see listed as the most effective ways to develop student maturity and perseverance.

I have one quibble with the authors: The appendices should be front and centre and in the main body of the text – they are that meaty. Take it from someone who has read this entire book: There is so much substance and practical wisdom in these appendices that you don't want to treat them as anything less than required reading. Sometimes we read education books and skip the appendices until we flip through them later in the year when we need their information; I'm telling you, if you do this, you'll regret it. Give the appendices your full attention and get ready for the great conversations with colleagues and students they'll inspire.

The specifics may be the greatest benefit of this book. I don't think I've ever read an assessment/reporting education book with as many real classroom examples of the authors' ideas in action as I find here. And the education technology connections fly off the page! It's dangerous, of course, to recommend specific apps and software in a book because the moment the book is published, some of those apps and software have already been replaced by new versions or something entirely different. Yes, we get practical use right now, but the greater benefit of these sections in the years of readership ahead (even if that software doesn't exist) is the catalyst to really look at what's available technically that will boost the successful incorporation of all these assessment principles and practices in our classrooms. It also gives us conviction to get our priorities right: We first determine our pedagogy, then find tech to support it. We do not limit our pedagogy because we have no tech to do it. Dream big, say Herbst and Davies, and readers will too.

Some educators will claim that we can get away with some of these ideas and outcomes-based assessments and their related practices in elementary school, but when the stakes are much higher in secondary levels, we have to get serious and stop using them. It won't serve students well in the working world or when they apply to universities, they say. Here's the reality check, however: These practices work just as well in high school, and they are more preparatory for post-high school work and education than more traditional practices that don't use them. And just as important, assessment and reporting at elementary levels can have as high an impact as assessment and reporting in high schools. Again, futures are built or destroyed by assessment and reporting practices at all levels, so this has to be done correctly. Herbst and Davies know this: Even though they are friendly in tone, there are no simplistic platitudes or sugary solutions here.

We want practices that are researched based, but to be honest, not all that is wise and wonderful in education has a strong research base. As a profession, we're still working on that. Herbst and Davies, however, come as close as possible to providing, not only the practical know-how, but also the research to back it up. They are intimate with the behind-the-scenes thinking, but also with the larger picture of what it means to implement. They treat us as professionals, empowering each of us, even presenting research at one point that states, "Teachers' informed professional judgment in relation to a comprehensive collection of evidence can be more reliable and valid than external test results." Wow, that's validating! For some, it's also a bit scary.

Don't worry because you've got Herbst and Davies walking side by side with you. You're well-equipped and thoughtfully guided. Watch your students soar!

Rick Wormeli
Teacher, Teacher Trainer, and Author of *Fair Isn't Always Equal: Assessment and Grading in the Differentiated Classroom*

Introduction

"Always walk through life as if you have something new to learn and you will."
Vernon Howard

No matter how many times a teacher may have written report cards, we still hear that preparing to write them is a time of anxiety and uncertainty. *"Do I have enough information about this student?", "What will the parents think when they read this?", "Will my principal think that my comments are good enough?", "What does the rating scale on this new report really mean?"* These questions, along with countless others, are not really a surprise, since educators, parents, *and* students are currently experiencing significant cognitive dissonance surrounding evaluation and reporting. Informed grading and reporting today is different from the grading and reporting that educators used during the twentieth century, because of issues such as what counts as reliable and valid evidence, how teachers can get it all done and done well while still having a life, or whether or not to assign zeros.

Successfully responding to the challenging task of informed reporting today is possible only when methods unique to classroom assessment are properly implemented. Done well, classroom evaluation and reporting:

- reflect a student's consistent and recent pattern of performance in relation to agreed-upon standards, criteria, and predetermined levels of quality

- occur after students have been involved in understanding quality by co-constructing criteria and *after* students have had the time and opportunity to learn

- take place in relation to the full range of educational standards or outcomes and is based upon a wide array of evidence of learning selected because of its alignment with outcomes and standards

- are understood by students (both expectations and acceptable evidence) and are derived from evidence present, not absent

- do not reflect data related to factors such as effort, attitude, attendance, and punctuality, which are evaluated and reported separately using the "Learning Skills" or "Work Habits" portion of the report card

- reflects informed teacher professional judgment of the level of quality of student work in relation to the criteria of success given the learning standards and outcomes

- takes place in an environment where there are quality-assurance and control processes that are validated and anchored in collaborative conversation and analysis of student work against agreed-upon criteria by teachers, and across grade levels and subjects – in order to ensure consistency and fairness in judgment

Effective classroom assessment supports learning and leads to quality reporting that respects the structure of each unique subject area, supports student learning and achievement, communicates effectively with a range of audiences, and fulfills teachers' required legal and regulatory responsibilities. There is no single right answer to the challenge of quality evaluation and reporting but rather many right answers that reflect the subject being taught and the ways of learning and knowing that students need to demonstrate.

The essential components of *Grading, Reporting, and Professional Judgment in Elementary Classrooms* both model and mirror effective practice: preparing for learning, teaching, and assessment; engaging students in assessment in support of their learning; and reporting the learning to others.

Preparing to teach means preparing for students to learn. Within an instructional framework, it involves identifying what comes *before.* For our purposes, we organize the *before* around the following four professional and instructional responsibilities when teachers:

- determine the learning destination

- research the expected quality levels

- plan to collect reliable and valid evidence of learning

- collect baseline evidence of learning

What happens *during* the learning calls us to constantly adjust, revise, and refine based on a continuous flow of information feedback. As we activate and engage our learners, teachers:

- describe the learning destination and expected quality

- involve students and provide time and support for them to learn

- teach to student needs based on assessment evidence

- collect reliable and valid evidence of learning

Then, *at the end of learning*, we evaluate the degree to which learning has occurred and report that to others. This requires that teachers:

- finalize the collection of evidence of learning
- make informed professional judgments
- report learning and achievement using the required format
- involve students in the reporting process

This instructional framework – which includes before, during, and after – is both familiar and powerful, and a proven practice in achieving informed classroom assessment, evaluation, and reporting. In each section of this book – preparing, engaging, and reporting – you will find the specifics of what needs to be done to successfully implement assessment, evaluation, and grading and reporting, using your professional judgment. There are numerous examples from a wide range of subject areas, including science, mathematics, social studies, and English language arts.

Let's begin by defining important terms relating to classroom assessment. Note that the terms *assessment* and *evaluation* need to be carefully used because they mean different things. Assessment occurs when teachers observe and coach students as they practise and learn. Assessment, at the classroom level, is sometimes referred to as *formative assessment*, particularly when the information that arises is used to inform instruction. Evaluation is the "show time"; it happens at the end of the practice. Assessment occurs *during* the learning, while evaluation occurs at the end of the learning.

To illustrate, let's consider two classroom accounts:

In March, Joshua, a Kindergarten student, was asked by his teacher to put a blue sticky note somewhere on his most recent self-portrait. He was to carefully select an aspect of his self-portrait that he knew he had done better this time than previous times. He placed the blue sticky note right on top of the mid-section. When asked why he did that, he responded that in all the other pictures, his arms and legs had come straight out of his head. This time, though, they were coming out of his body. In order to prove this, he got out of his chair and crouched low to the ground so that it looked like his arms and legs were coming out of his head and said, "See…just like this. This is how I used to draw!"

While this anecdote can bring a smile, it is also a great example of assessment in action. The student himself is telling his teacher what he has learned and what he is now better able to do. He views himself as a learner who is capable and in charge of his next steps. Some might say that Joshua's realization should have come before the month of March and, as a result, he is lagging behind in his development. That statement moves us into the realm of evaluation – the time when his teacher would use professional judgment to determine the degree to which his learning is meeting developmental milestones and expectations.

Let's move to a Grade 8 classroom where the students and teacher examined several lab report structures and established criteria for "What counts in a quality lab report?" Because the teacher and the students have worked together to co-construct the criteria, the description of quality is comprehensive and complete. Each of the three criteria (and their commensurate details) are colour-coded. The next time the students were asked to submit their lab reports, they were also expected to prove, using the different colours, that they incorporated the elements that the criteria identified. The teacher returned the lab reports, including specific, descriptive feedback that related to the criteria, and highlighted areas for further improvement. After a time to revise, the students re-submitted their work and the teacher scored the reports using the criteria as the language of the "4" on the rubric scale.

Notice the similarity of this account to the one from Kindergarten. Students were deeply involved in the assessment process; they were central to the examination of samples, to the creation of criteria, and to proving that their work was in alignment with the criteria. They were able to easily engage in self-assessment. The teacher provided another layer of feedback, and only after time had been given to refine the work, did the teacher move to the evaluative stance; she used her professional judgment to determine the degree to which the lab reports now met the stated level of quality and proficiency.

These two accounts help us to better understand the difference between *assessment* and *evaluation*. This difference makes even further sense if you consider the etymology of the words in English. The root of *assessment* is the word *assess*, which means "to sit beside." The root of the word *evaluation* is *value*, which means "to judge." So, when we assess, ". . . we are gathering information about student learning that informs our teaching and helps students learn more. . . . When we evaluate, we decide whether or not students have learned what they needed to learn and how well they have learned it. Evaluation is a process of reviewing the evidence and determining its value" (Davies, 2011, p. 1). It is especially important to understand that when classroom-based assessment is done well, it leads to further learning and to clarity of communication about learning and achievement. Grading decisions become accurate reflections of learning.

The Assessment Reform Group (2002) and Stiggins (2002) coined two additional terms that have supported a deeper understanding of classroom assessment: *Assessment for Learning* and *Assessment of Learning*. Assessment *for* learning is formative assessment, plus the deep involvement of learners in the assessment process. Assessment *of* learning is the same as summative assessment, or evaluation. When assessment *for* learning is done well, teachers have the information they need to teach to emerging needs so all students are learning *and* students have the information they need to self-regulate and self-monitor their way to success. When assessment *of* learning is done well, teachers' informed professional judgment is more reliable and more valid than external tests (ARG, 2006; Burger et al., 2009). See Figure I-1 below for the difference between large-scale and classroom assessment.

Figure I-1 ▼

Large-Scale and Classroom Assessment – What's the Difference?

	Large-Scale Assessment	Classroom Assessment
Purpose	To account for the achievement of groups of students in relation to the learning outcomes	To account for the learning and achievement of individual students
Research Question	What is the pattern and trend for groups of students at different points in the system?	Does this student know, apply, and articulate what he/she needs to know, do, and articulate given curriculum expectations?
Audience	The larger community as well as every part of the school system that works in support of student learning.	The primary audience is students and their parents with the secondary audience being the school and school system.
Reliability (Explanation: Your findings are repeatable – that is, they are collected over time day-by-day and you observe students creating evidence of learning. You actually witness students knowing, doing, and articulating what they need to know, do, or articulate over time.)	Large-scale assessment has procedures to check for reliability.	Classroom assessment collects similar information (data) over time so that what a student knows, can do, and can articulate is evidenced through products, observations, and conversations.
Validity (Explanation: You are assessing what you are supposed to assess and the evidence of learning is collected from multiple sources over time (a process of triangulation).)	Validity can be thought about in a variety of ways. Because of the amount of information collected through large-scale assessment, the findings are valid at the group level.	Validity, when it comes to classroom assessment, is often focused on the match of the evidence of learning to the learning expectations, as expressed in the relevant documents.

© Herbst, S. and Davies, A. (2014) *A Fresh Look at Grading and Reporting in High Schools*, p. xviii.

In our work, *professional judgment* can be defined as, and is informed by, one's knowledge of context, pedagogy, child development, reliable and valid evidence of learning, methods of collecting that evidence of learning, and the criteria and standards that describe success. Holding a valid teacher's certificate does not mean that we, as educators, automatically and in perpetuity, have informed professional judgment. Rather, "in professional practice, judgment involves a purposeful and systematic thinking process that evolves in terms and accuracy and insight with ongoing reflection and self-correction" (Ministry of Education, Ontario, 2010, p. 152).

Step-by-step, this book describes how you can effectively work through complexity to something much, much better – that is, a powerful, practical, and informed grading and reporting process. Our goal is to express complex ideas in a set of easy-to-do steps, using straightforward language. However, do not be deceived by the simplicity of the ideas we share. Alfred North Whitehead once wrote, "...the only simplicity to be trusted is the simplicity to be found on the far side of complexity." We have found that it is only when we truly understand the complexity of grading, reporting, and professional judgment that we can begin to take practical next steps towards positive change.

This look at grading, reporting, and professional judgment arises from the important work of transforming classroom assessment, and results from our work over many years alongside elementary teachers, as well as school and system leaders. Proven practices do not stand still; rather, they evolve when teachers, schools, and systems seek to respond positively to questions and issues. And so, we thank all the educators who have helped us take away anything unnecessary that might lie between a teacher and successful classroom assessment practice.

This book is also meant for those of you in leadership roles: principals, assistant principals, district personnel, directors, and superintendents. It is important that you, too, understand these ideas. Teachers need your support. They must believe that you "have their backs" as they do what is right for their students' learning.

If you are a middle school teacher and find yourself in greater alignment with secondary reporting structures, we might suggest that you read the companion book to this one – *A Fresh Look at Grading and Reporting in High School* (Herbst & Davies, 2014).

We trust that these student-, teacher-, administrator-, and parent-tested ideas will help you find your way to grading and reporting processes that are both possible and practical in your context, so that your actions support student learning and help you to have a life beyond the classroom – not just during report card time, but all year long.

That's it. It is as simple (and as complex) as that.

Let's get started.

> *"The illiterate of the 21st century will not be those who cannot read and write, but those who cannot learn, unlearn, and relearn."*
> *Alvin Toffler*

Preparing for Quality Classroom Assessment

"The person doing the work is the one growing the dendrites."

Pat Wolfe

Report cards seem to be always changing. Yet, some things never really change. The process of reporting student progress and growth begins at the start of the school year and is refined with the beginning of each new term. It is true that if you know where you are going you are more likely to get there. So, taking time to determine just what students are expected to learn – knowledge, understanding, application, and articulation – means that we can better ensure that the evidence of learning we collect is what we need in order to be certain that our professional judgment is reliable and valid. And, as we research appropriate quality levels, we come to understand development over time in relation to expectations, which informs our professional judgment. The result is teachers have more of the information needed in order to coach all students – wherever they are in their learning – towards success and expected proficiency levels.

As teachers review what needs to be learned and the quality levels expected, they begin to select the tasks, activities, assignments, and learning events that will scaffold the learning and create the evidence needed to demonstrate that learning. Then, as the kind of evidence is determined, teachers can plan ways to collect the needed observations, products, and conversations. This is also the time when teachers begin to consider what evidence of learning *students* can collect.

CONTENTS

Preparation for student learning begins with planning for quality classroom assessment. There are four areas to consider:

1. determining the learning destination
2. researching the expected quality levels
3. planning to collect reliable and valid evidence of learning
4. collecting baseline evidence of learning

1. Determining the Learning Destination

For most teachers, figuring out what standards or outcomes need to be taught (and learned by students) is harder than it sounds. It is not simply a matter of turning to the curriculum documents, lists of core competencies, or standards. Ideally, teachers need to be masters of their discipline(s); this is difficult when they begin their careers or are teaching outside their discipline, getting new teaching assignments each year, or in the case of elementary education, being simultaneously responsible for teaching in multiple subject areas. Whether teachers are masters of their discipline or not, they need to plan to be successful; they need to begin with the end in mind.

Consider this process (see Figure 1-1):

- Choose one subject area. You might want to think about one term or unit

- Download or copy the standards or outcomes that students are to learn and cut them into individual chunks. (This process helps you use more than just one of your senses, which is helpful in learning.)

- Organize the standards or learning outcomes into groupings that make sense to you by sorting the individual statements related to a topic, concept, or process.

- When the groupings are finalized, summarize each group by identifying a "big idea" so the standards or outcomes can be shared with others in simple, clear, student-friendly language that corresponds to how the learning needs to be reported later.

- Return and review the standards and outcomes in their original form. Check back to see if there is anything you have missed.

- Ask colleagues to review your draft using a protocol that facilitates specific, descriptive feedback (see samples on pages 11 and 12).

- Make revisions based on the results of the protocol conversation.

Figure 1-1 ▼

Grade 3 Mathematics

Listing of content and process outcomes

Organized groups identified by "big ideas"

This is a deceptively simple process. It is important to group the standards or outcomes so you can see what parts you will teach together. This will often enable you to address multiple standards or learning outcomes in any given time period - an efficient way to proceed.

Your grouping will be unique to you and will reflect your understanding of the subject area. It is helpful to involve a trusted colleague to review your work and give comments about parts you might have missed or underemphasized. Remembering and sharing four or five big ideas with others makes sense; sharing 150 or more separate standards or outcomes is simply overwhelming for everyone.

Teachers do need to know all the standards and outcomes because they are responsible for teaching them. When teachers group standards and describe them in student-friendly language that describes quality, everyone's understanding increases. This is one of the first steps teachers take in preparing to teach students to monitor their own learning; it helps them understand what they need to learn. And we know that engaging students in this process supports self-regulation and executive functioning. (See Figures 1-2 and 1-3 for additional examples.)

▼ **Figure 1-2**

Writing: Intermediate and Primary Examples

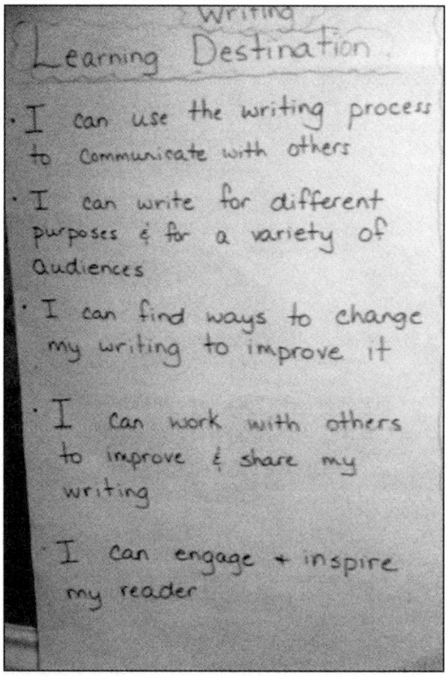

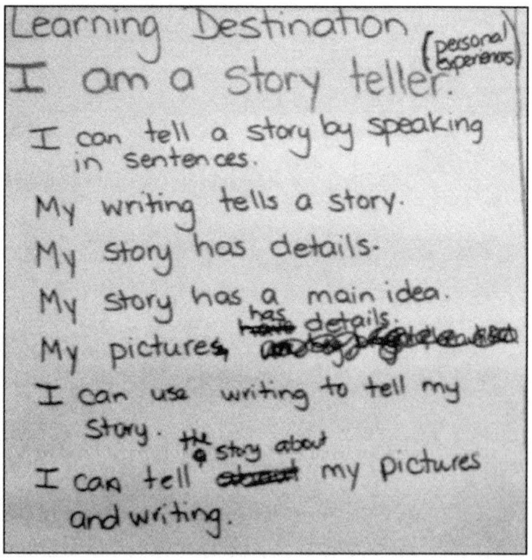

Figure 1-3 ▼

Teachers engaged in this work need to take into account both what needs to be learned and how the learning needs to be reported. Descriptions of learning destinations vary from place to place because the contexts differ. Therefore, it is important that we work through this process collaboratively across grade levels to draft student-friendly descriptions of learning destinations. When teachers work together, these descriptions are informed through their collective expertise. As a result, everyone is better prepared to communicate with all partners in the school community. Also, when draft versions of learning destinations are shared among colleagues, everyone can improve and build upon the work. Everyone saves time while building confidence in the accuracy, clarity, and usefulness of the final drafts.

Science Example

- I can make connections between different concepts in both science + other subjects
- I can relate subject matter to real life situations
- I can understand my role + responsibilities as a scientist and apply myself towards good stewardship of the people + world around me.
- I can understand + articulate concepts with other students

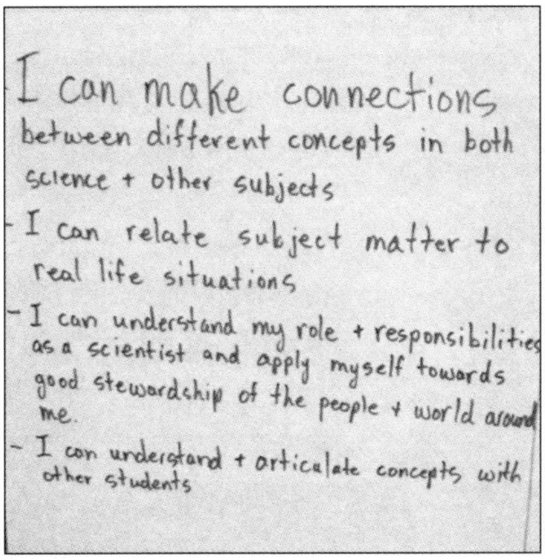

Once the standards and learning outcomes are grouped so they make sense, given the subject area and grade level, and teachers have written them in language their students are able to understand, it is time to bring full meaning to the words through researching the expected quality and achievement levels given grade expectations.

2. Researching the Expected Quality Levels

It is hard to know what quality or proficiency actually is. It is true that curricular standards or learning outcomes define what students need in order to learn, be able to do, and be able to articulate, but these standards do not show what it looks like when they do. For example, "communicates effectively in writing" looks different for a seven-year-old, a 16-year-old, or a 36-year-old. Teachers may know what the learning standard is, but they may need support to understand what it looks like for students of a particular age or in a particular discipline. And, if teachers are not clear about what reaching success looks like for their students, they will not know when their students have reached it.

Being able to recognize quality and success is an important part of professional judgment. There are ways that teachers can inform their professional judgment. For example, research has shown that comparing student work to samples or criteria improves teachers' professional judgment (ARG, 2006; Burger et al., 2009). Teachers can gather collections of samples that illustrate the standard or learning outcome from work in progress, from collections available online, or from colleagues.

When teachers analyze samples together using a protocol, they build common understandings and collective agreements about expectations of quality and achievement for different subject areas and grade levels. While teachers in the past may have learned about quality in informal ways, today it is done with intention. More and more often, teachers deliberately work together to share teaching expertise and to come to a common understanding of quality work. Conversations among colleagues are informed by:

- examining samples of student work for particular assignments or tasks
- looking at collections of student work to show development over time
- considering results of common assessments and performance tasks
- analyzing external assessment data

Looking at Samples of Student Work

When teachers work together to look at samples of student work, select those that best represent expected levels of quality for assignments or tasks, then go further and develop criteria, rubrics, or developmental continua, they deepen their understanding of what quality is and what the expectations for a particular subject or grade level are. Samples and exemplar collections can take many forms, including maps, reading responses, science lab reports, writing projects, mathematical problems, videos of oral presentations, musical performances, computer animations, and research projects. Teachers can consider anything that illustrates what students are expected to know, do, and articulate in relation to their learning. (See Figure 1-4 for an example of teachers gathering and using samples.)

Criteria are a description of what quality and proficiency actually look like. Once teachers have determined which samples will best illustrate quality work and grade-level

Figure 1-4 ▼

An Example of Teachers Gathering and Using Samples

With thanks to Mililani 'Ike Elementary School, Hawai'i.

expectations, it is important that they continue to work together to create criteria, rubrics, or developmental continua. This process builds the language of quality.

For example, teachers may have collected samples from across curricular areas that illustrate a high level of critical thinking. Together, they identify criteria that describes, in words, a complete picture of what critical thinking actually is and the ways that it can be iterated in student work. (See Figure 1-5a for a four-step process to use and Figure 1-5b for an example of criteria regarding the competency of critical thinking.)

Rubrics can be useful to determine a mark or a score based on a description of quality and the "shades" of quality. However, they are often not well-crafted for use in the classroom, particularly with young

Figure 1-5a ▼

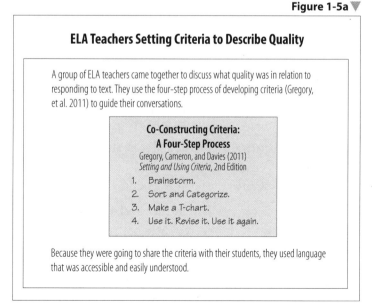

ELA Teachers Setting Criteria to Describe Quality

A group of ELA teachers came together to discuss what quality was in relation to responding to text. They use the four-step process of developing criteria (Gregory, et al. 2011) to guide their conversations.

Co-Constructing Criteria:
A Four-Step Process
Gregory, Cameron, and Davies (2011)
Setting and Using Criteria, 2nd Edition
1. Brainstorm.
2. Sort and Categorize.
3. Make a T-chart.
4. Use it. Revise it. Use it again.

Because they were going to share the criteria with their students, they used language that was accessible and easily understood.

Criteria – Critical Thinking

children. It is important that teachers who choose to use rubrics with students consider their purpose carefully. Is the rubric to support learning and improvement? Or, is the rubric to evaluate and score student work?

One way to improve a rubric is to:

- Ensure each level describes what success, not failure, looks like.

- Ensure the language in each section describes what is working – what the student is able to do (not what they can't do).

- Ensure the rubric describes, not the errors that have been made, but rather what the student needs to do to move to the next level.

- Ensure each level shows the next steps for students so they can move from where they are to where they are going.

- If possible, student work samples are available to illustrate the changes in quality from level to level and between each level.

In the early years, rubric levels are often accompanied by exemplars that visually illustrate what the words of the rubric are intending to communicate. (See Figure 1-6.) For many students, and especially for those who struggle, the gap or step between what a "1" and a "2" looks like or what a "2" and a "3" looks like can be overwhelming and difficult to navigate. For this reason, those who teach very young students shift from rubrics to visual continua to show what the very next step looks like – not just the next scoring level.

Engaging in the creation of these visual progressions informs teachers' professional judgment; they are comparing their assessment of different samples of student work with their colleagues' assessments of the same samples. Teachers use moderated processes to organize samples from the least developed to the most sophisticated, with each progressive sample differing from the previous one in just one or two attributes or characteristics.

Figure 1-6 ▼

An Example of Teachers Gathering and Using Samples

With thanks to Erin Clarke, Manitoba.

In all of these examples, the opportunity to talk with colleagues about differences in professional judgments gives everyone the chance to develop a shared understanding of what quality and expectations look like.

▼ **Figure 1-7**

Shared Understanding of Quality and Expectations in English Language Arts		
I consistently and independently listen, speak, read, write, view, and represent to:	I have evidence that shows proof of learning…	These samples help show that quality includes…
Students will listen, speak, read, write, view and represent to:	Products, observations and conversations from ELA and other subject areas.	Activities and tasks result in evidence that can be used as proof of learning. Along the way it can be used to inform day-by-day teaching.
General Outcome 1: …explore thoughts, ideas, feelings and experiences. 1.1 Discover and explore 1.2 Clarify and extend	• Reader response journal • Observations from small group work • Writing folder • Photographs of 3-D work as well as presentations	• Read and respond daily to choice reading materials • Talk in small groups (lit circles/readers club) • Write daily – writers workshop • Class meetings • Conflict resolution center
General Outcome 2: …comprehend and respond personally and critically to oral, print and other media texts. 2.1 Use strategies and cues 2.2 Respond to texts 2.3 Understand forms, elements and techniques 2.4 Create original text	• Reader response journal entries: include responses during choice reading time, responses to text or media (whole group and choice), responses to required reading, as well as practice assignments • Observations of small group work • Observations of individuals • Writing/Representing portfolio (includes choice writing and required exercises) • Photographs of 3-D work as well as presentations	• Read and respond daily to teacher selected materials, including texts read aloud/materials viewed • Practice reading strategies (whole class/small group/individual) • Read aloud daily • Daily focused lesson and individual practice • Write daily using writers' workshop (deliberately use text structures in writing and storyboard structures in viewing)
General Outcome 3: …manage ideas and information. 3.1 Plan and focus 3.2 Select and process 3.3 Organize, record and evaluate 3.4 Share and review	• See evidence listed in assessment plans for Science and Social Studies • Literature projects (criteria)	• Projects and tasks connected to Science or Social Studies topic • Literature projects (If you are not self-contained then you must provide time in each term to focus on a learning and students producing evidence that addresses this general outcome)
General Outcome 4: …enhance the clarity and artistry of communication. 4.1 Enhance and improve 4.2 Attend to conventions 4.3 Present and share	• Daily oral reading record/observations • Presentations of work to partners and small groups (observations in relation to criteria) • Video and audio presentations (recordings) • Presentation to parents and family (at home performance) (feedback form) • Daily Edit (conventions)	• Daily reading • Presenting work (during and end) • Small group work • Video/audio presentations • Presentations to parents and others • Daily Edits • Writing & Representing Folder
General Outcome 5: …respect, support and collaborate with others. 5.1 Respect others and strengthen community 5.2 Work within a group	• Group meetings (criteria) • Partner work (criteria checklist) • Small group work (criteria checklist) • Conflict resolution center (log notes) • Big buddies (criteria)	• Group meetings • Partner work • Small group work • Conflict resolution center • Big buddies

Looking at Collections of Student Work

Another way to research the expected levels of quality is to examine entire collections of student work. Because teachers need to arrive at a well-informed professional judgment, it is important that they examine all the evidence of learning collected in relation to all the standards and learning outcomes upon which the report card grades are based. Looking at samples of just one or two pieces of student work is often not enough.

Collections of student work can be complex and can vary from student to student; therefore, teachers need to develop a common understanding of the many different "looks" of quality in relation to subject area curricula or grade-level expectations. There are a variety of protocols available to inform this work. (See Figure 1-7 for an example of a description of quality in ELA based on looking at collections of student work. See Figure 1-8 and Figure 1-9 for sample protocols.)

Figure 1-8 ▼

SALT Protocol

A group of teachers worked together to redefine success in their classes. They moved from being grades-based on assignments, tests, quizzes, and participation to defining quality based on the evidence of learning in relation to course standards. Partway through the course, they asked students to review the evidence of learning that they had generated. Students put together the best collection of evidence they had that demonstrated that they were successfully meeting course outcomes. The teacher selected one student's collection of evidence that met the quality description. He brought it to the working session. As the colleagues gathered, they used a protocol that required a close examination of the evidence of learning. They commented on how it did (or did not yet) meet the quality expectations as defined. The presenting teacher was able to listen to his colleagues exercise their professional judgment in relation to the collection of evidence and consider how their comments were similar (or not).

Agreement about Quality

1. Appoint a timekeeper and facilitator. Begin.
2. The presenting teacher describes the evidence. (2 minutes)
3. Three reviewers ask questions to clarify. (3 minutes)
4. Group members review the work. They discuss the work in relation to excellence (e.g., A) while the presenting teacher listens. (5-7 minutes)
5. The presenting teacher joins the conversation and points out anything that might have been missed. (2 minutes)
6. Each participant sums up by commenting on where they think the evidence is in relation to excellence. (5 minutes)
7. The presenting teacher reflects on the process. The group reflects on the process. (5 minutes)
8. Repeat the process with another teacher presenting another body of evidence for one student.

Do You See What I See?

Purpose of the Protocol: to learn from what others see in the student work. By listening fully to what others see in the student work a teacher may gain information about both the learning and the teaching. This Protocol may be used to address the question of validity of an assessment or an assignment by answering, "Does this assessment really assess what it intends to assess?"

Prior to the Conversation: The presenting teacher needs to select 3 samples of student work that represent a range of quality responses to the assignment or assessment. For confidentiality and to remove bias, student names are removed and the work is labeled Student A, Student B, and Student C. Copies of student work samples are made for everyone in the group.

(2 minutes) *Getting Started.* Select a facilitator and a timekeeper. Review the purpose of the Protocol and ground rules for this process.

(8 minutes) *Silent Reflection.* The presenting teacher distributes the student work. Nothing is said about the work, its context, or the students. The participants scan the work in silence, making notes about what they see in the learning).

(8 minutes) *Describing the Work.* The facilitator asks, "What did you see in the work?" Participants respond without judgment about the quality of the work and the evidence of learning that they see. If judgments emerge, the facilitator reminds the speaker to describe the evidence on which the judgment was made. The presenting teacher remains quiet and takes notes.

(8 minutes) *Raising Questions and Hunches.* The facilitator asks:
- What questions does this work raise for you?
- What do you think this student is working on?
- What did you learn about how this student thinks and learns?
- What do you think the teacher was attempting to assess?

Group members offer their questions and ideas. The presenting teacher remains quiet and takes notes.

(15 minutes) *Dialogue.* At the facilitator's invitation, the presenting teacher responds to anything learned from colleagues or any questions he/she wants to pursue. The facilitator asks:
- What new perspectives did you learn about student learning from your colleagues?
- What questions were raised that you may wish to pursue to improve the learning?
- Are there new ideas that you might like to try in your classroom?

The presenting teacher invites other colleagues into the discussion.

(5 minutes) *Reflection on the Conversation.* The group discusses how they experienced this conference and what they learned.

Adapted from the Collaborative Assessment Conference Protocol by the Coalition of Essential Schools.
Box 1969, Brown University, Providence, RI 02912.   www.essentialschools.org/

© Glaude, C. (2005) *Protocols for Professional Learning Conversations*, pp. 32, 33.

Considering Results of Common Assessments and Performance Tasks

Another way for teachers to research the expected levels of quality is to consider the results of high-quality common assessments – that is, to look at the evidence of learning that they have agreed to have their students create. This student work might be a performance task or it might be a collection of student work from a unit of study that has the same learning goals.

Once the student work has been collected, teachers meet and co-construct criteria and the accompanying rubric (or scoring guide), focusing on what is important; they look at what is quality in a particular product or process that comprises evidence of student learning. Teachers may choose to select samples that illustrate key aspects of learning across the different levels of the rubric. Anchor papers of student work – work that serves as an illustration of the different levels of the rubric – are annotated so that they clearly communicate and illustrate what students can do.

Teachers then score the set of student work using the rubric (or scoring guide) and anchor samples to guide their decision-making. They record their scores privately using sticky notes or by highlighting a copy of the rubric for each student work. Once teachers have finished scoring, they check for inter-rater reliability – that is, they look to see where their evaluations are similar and where they are different.

Where there are differences, discussions take place and group agreement is reached. If needed, the wording of the rubric is adjusted to better reflect the intended meaning. This process of looking together at student work using a common task, test, or body of evidence of student learning is a helpful beginning point for understanding the key components of quality work. It is not the end of the process, however.

If teacher learning stops here, informed professional judgment may continue to be elusive. It is important that teachers continue engaging in this process over time, continually checking for and further establishing common understandings of quality in relation to a particular grade level or subject area. (See Figure 1-10 for three examples of teacher conversations related to quality.)

▼ **Figure 1-10**

Teacher Conversations about Analyzing Student Samples to Inform Understanding of Quality

Example – Problem-solving in Mathematics: One K–8 school faculty was committed to exploring problem-solving in mathematics. Teachers gathered samples from all classes across the school. The K–3 students, the 4–6 students, and the 7–8 students each did a different task.

When the teachers gathered with the samples from their classes, six examples from each class showed the full range of the problem-solving being done by students. The teachers looked at samples and grouped them into one pile, regardless of age or grade level. Then, the one pile was divided quickly into three groups – early, along the way, advanced. The teachers were divided into groups to read and analyze the samples in each pile. As they looked at the work, they divided each pile into three more groups. Then, they changed working partners and analyzed yet more samples. By the end of their work time, they had 30 collections of two to three work samples across the K–9 grades that mapped out the progression in growth and understanding. Each sample had sticky notes that recorded statements about what was *present* in the work – not what was absent nor the degree to which it was present. The attribute was either there or not. Then, teachers worked together to describe the key features in terms of what was important about the samples at each level. Together, the samples and the words became a draft progression that they used in the following year to support learning by identifying what students were able to do and what they needed to do to improve.

This same process has been followed in many schools looking at different aspects of student learning. Schools have considered work samples such as writing development and recordings of students' oral reading over time. One jurisdiction, for example, collected photographs of student artwork over time. There are a growing number of collections available online, and these can be very useful. However, developing your own set with colleagues engages you directly in the process and helps you develop your own informed professional judgment. It is very worth doing.

Analyzing External Assessment Data to Inform Levels of Quality

One other way to research the expected levels of quality is to analyze external test results. This analysis provides teachers with an opportunity to consider where their students are experiencing success (and what they, therefore, want to continue doing more of) and determine where students are struggling. For example, if teachers have identified what they feel are appropriate levels of quality, and if they are making professional judgments of student work based on those levels of quality, they may decide that 90 percent of the students are meeting quality expectations. Then, when the external test results arrive and they indicate, for example, that only 40 percent of students are meeting quality expectations, teachers have a choice. They could dismiss the external test as invalid or they could examine the test and see what was emphasized. They could ask themselves whether or not they need to adjust not only what they emphasize, but also the ways that students need to communicate their understanding and the quality level expected. This conclusion, in response to the question "Do our quality expectations match external expectations?"

provides an opportunity to inform and clarify. (See Figure 1-11 for questions that we have used successfully when considering the results of external assessment data.)

Figure 1-11 ▼

Questions to Consider When Looking at External Assessment Data

Questions to use when analyzing external assessment data

1. What surprises you about the data?

2. What does not surprise you about the data?

3. What can this data tell us?

4. What does this data not tell us?

5. In what ways does this data represent this group of students?

6. In what ways does this data not represent this group of students?

7. How does this data compare to groups of students from this school in the past?

8. How does this data compare to the district average? State average? Provincial average?

9. We have put in place some interventions over the past year. This data tells us that what we have been doing is working well in these ways…is not working well in these ways….What are some implications for action?

10. As we look at the data for our school over the past five years, we are doing better/worse/the same as before. What are your hunches about why this might be so?

11. What patterns and trends are emerging for you as you look at this data?

12. What patterns and trends are emerging for you as you look at the data over the past several years?

13. Specifically, what areas of strength are you noticing for this group of students?

14. Specifically, what areas of challenge are you noticing for this group of students?

15. What can we learn about what we are doing well as a department?

16. What can we learn about areas of challenge for us as a department?

17. What areas might we need to focus on in the next year/next semester?

18. Who might we need to enlist in order to more closely understand what this data is telling us?

19. What is this data telling us about sub-groups of our students (e.g., gender, ethnicity)?

© Herbst, S. and Davies, A. (2014) *A Fresh Look at Grading and Reporting in High Schools*, p. 12.

In summary, teachers' and students' future success can be thoughtfully supported through structured conversations, discussions, and learning. Over time, the result of these conversations is the development of commonly held levels of quality in relation to standards or learning outcomes. There are numerous resources to support this kind of work (e.g., Dufour et al., 2006; Glaude, 2005, 2010).

3. Planning to Collect Reliable and Valid Evidence of Learning

The next part of developing an effective assessment plan is to identify potential activities, tasks, projects, and other learning events that will result in evidence of learning.

Classroom assessment is a research-based inquiry process that has its roots in social science. Evidence of learning matters. As you work, it is important to take care when gathering evidence of learning for a particular subject area. When evidence of learning is collected from multiple sources over time (products, observations, and conversations), it is referred to as triangulation (Lincoln and Guba, 1984). The evidence can be, potentially, as diverse as the students, teachers, and the various disciplines being taught. When evidence of learning is collected from multiple sources over time in relation to the learning destination, trends and patterns become apparent. This process can serve to increase the reliability and validity of teachers' professional judgment. Research clearly shows that teachers' informed professional judgment, in relation to a comprehensive collection of evidence, can be more reliable and valid than external test results (ARG, 2006; Burger et al., 2009). It takes some planning for teachers to make sure that they have enough evidence, the right kinds of evidence, and evidence that is reliable and valid.

Once teachers have analyzed the outcomes and standards, determined what students need to learn, and have developed a sense of what success might look like for their students, it is time for them to consider what kinds of evidence of learning will need to be collected. This planning process not only informs instruction but also ensures validity and reliability. If teachers attend to validity and reliability while undertaking assessment in the classroom, then when it comes time to evaluate at the end of the learning period, they can be confident that they have the evidence they need in order to make informed, high-quality, and accurate professional judgments. (See Figure 1-12 for more information about reliability and validity.)

Teachers can easily be overwhelmed by all the potential evidence of learning that they could be collecting in relation to the standards or learning outcomes. Think about the key activities, tasks, projects, and other learning opportunities; the list of evidence of learning seems endless. And, if you consider all the various ways that students might best show proof of their learning, especially given access to technology tools, this list gets impossibly

Figure 1-12

Reliable and Valid Professional Judgment	
Your professional judgment is more reliable if…	Your professional judgment is more likely to be valid if…
• your findings are repeatable, that is, they are collected over time day-by-day and you observe students creating evidence of learning. • you actually witness students knowing, doing, and articulating what they need to know, do, or articulate over time.	• you are assessing what you are supposed to assess and the evidence of learning is collected from multiple sources over time (a process of triangulation).

© Herbst, S. and Davies, A. (2014) *A Fresh Look at Grading and Reporting in High Schools*, p. 13.

long. How does one make sense of it? When teachers take time to plan the evidence of learning that they need in order to be confident that their evaluation is both reliable and valid, their work becomes manageable.

Consider the best evidence of learning at the classroom level, given the subject area and grade-level standards, and make an assessment plan. After all, to be successful, you need to plan from the beginning so that students can create the evidence and then collect it. This helps you prepare to respond to the questions students often ask: "What counts? How much is it worth?"

Teachers often ask, "Given the standards and outcomes, what is the best evidence of learning? How much is enough?" When teachers have come to an understanding of what is to be learned in a unit or term, they can then determine the type of evidence best suited for students to show what they know, are able to do, and can articulate. Further, when teachers are seen to value all evidence of learning – both qualitative and quantitative – then students come to understand that everything they do, say, and create is potentially evidence of learning. This stance has the potential to change everything – from relationships, to motivation, to learning – because suddenly every moment, every action, every creation is of value. We evaluate what we value. What is valued then guides teaching and the collection of evidence of learning. (See Figures 1-13 and 1-14 for lists of evidence.)

Evidence of Learning for One Term in ELA

Proof of Learning in relation to Learning Outcomes	Learning Outcomes
• Observations from small group work • Writing folder • Photographs of 3-D work as well as presentations • Reader response journal entries -include responses during choice reading time, responses to text or media (whole group and choice), responses to required reading, as well as practice assignments • Observations of individuals • Writing/Representing portfolio (includes choice writing and required exercises) • Photographs of 3-D work as well as presentations • See evidence listed in assessment plans for Science and Social Studies • Literature projects (criteria) • Daily oral reading record/observations • Presentations of work to partners and small groups (observations in relation to criteria) • Video and audio presentations (recordings) • Presentation to parents and family (at home performance) (feedback form) • Daily edit (conventions) • Group meetings (criteria) • Partner work (criteria checklist) • Small group work (criteria checklist) • Conflict resolution center (log notes) • Big buddies (criteria)	Students will listen, speak, read, write, view and represent to: General Outcome 1: ... explore thoughts, ideas, feeling and experiences. 1.1 Discover and explore 1.2 Clarify and extend General Outcome 2: ... comprehend and respond personally and critically to oral, print and other media texts. 2.1 Use strategies and cues 2.2 Respond to texts 2.3 Understand forms, elements and techniques 2.4 Create original text General Outcome 3: ... manage ideas and information. 3.1 Plan and focus 3.2 Select and process 3.3 Organize, record and evaluate 3.4 Share and review General Outcome 4: ... enhance the clarity and artistry of communication. 4.1 Enhance and improve 4.2 Attend to conventions 4.3 Present and share General Outcome 5: ... respect, support and collaborate with others. 5.1 Respect others and strengthen community 5.2 Work within a group

▼ Figure 1-14

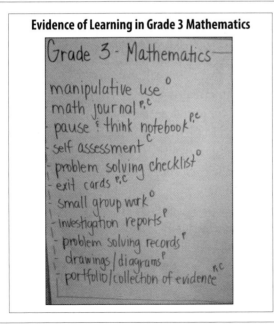

Evidence of Learning in Grade 3 Mathematics

When we begin with the end in mind and bring that clarity, not only to ourselves but our students regarding what they need to know, are able to do, and to articulate, we set everyone up for success. When teachers understand what quality looks like, they can plan to encourage students to represent what they know in different ways, while still being fair and equitable. For example, if the curriculum standard states that students should be able to "describe the water cycle and the impact of climate change on the water cycle," they could research and write about it, they could draw a mind map, they

18   CHAPTER 1   *www.connect2learning.com*

could create a digital presentation with visuals to illustrate their understanding, they could interview a scientist and annotate the transcript, or they could use newspaper and magazine clippings to illustrate key ideas. The expected learning does not change, but what students can do to demonstrate their learning in relation to the standard can be different. This is a key concept for ensuring that all students have the opportunity to show what they have learned.

As teachers become more knowledgeable about the implications of various theories of intelligence and ways of knowing, experience a greater diversity of students, and seek to meet the needs of the learners, they are expanding the ways that students show or represent what they know. It is essential that our assessment practices be equitable. It is also essential that our assessments be accurate reflections of learning. Treating students equally can be unfair. For example, when students are asked to represent what they know in social studies only in writing, some will be unable to do so due to their lack of writing skills. However, when asked to demonstrate, illustrate, or give an oral presentation, their knowledge and skill may rapidly become apparent (as will gaps in understanding).

What is the effect of this thinking within a subject area? Here is an example depicting how teachers can help students to show their learning in different ways. (See Figure 1-15.)

Over time, as teachers and students learn more about various ways of representing their learning, the list grows. Consider the three general sources of evidence of learning gathered in classrooms: observations of learning, the products that students create, and conversations between teachers and students.

Figure 1-15 ▼

List of Possible Ways to Show What You Know

Different ways to show what we know...

- draw a diagram
- make a time line
- make a poster
- write a story
- do an oral presentation
- write a poem
- build a model
- design a Web page
- create a puzzle
- make a video
- create an iMovie
- make a podcast

- make a recording
- design a T-shirt
- do a report
- write a song
- create a collage
- build a diorama
- write a play
- do a journal entry
- perform a puppet show
- input e-journal entry

© Davies, A. (2011) *Making Classroom Assessment Work*, 3rd Edition, p. 49.

Observations of Learning

The list of evidence teachers plan to collect in relation to the standards or outcomes for a subject or grade level needs to include the observations they will make while students are engaged in key processes related to the discipline being taught. Consider your standards or outcomes. Which of these can only be observed?

▼ Figure 1-16

Possible Observations in Oral Reading

Oral Reading – Grade 1

Learning Outcome: development of oral reading skills is an age-appropriate learning expectation for primary children

Evidence of Learning: peer reading, large group reading, presentations, readers theatre, poetry reading, home program, and individual reading

Observations: speed, expression, fluency, punctuation, self-correction, and word attack strategies such as skip reading, syllabication, picture clues, blending, and predicting

Report Comments for Oral Reading

Independent reader: reads a passage from an age-appropriate text with meaningful expression

Developing reader: reads a passage from an age-appropriate text smoothly and is learning to pause at appropriate places

Emerging reader: reads a passage word by word

▼ Figure 1-17

Possible Observations in Mathematics Problem-solving

- Student behaviour when tackling a problem
- Use of manipulatives
- Independent gathering of math tools
- Following a math problem-solving process
- Finding/referring to anchor chart
- Videos of students solving math problems
- Students highlighting relevant information in math problems
- Application of problem-solving strategies
- Observation of mathematical habits of mind

The observations you make become evidence. Teachers might observe formal and informal presentations, the scientific method being applied, group or partner activities, planning and designing, persuading, giving opinions, following instructions, listening to others, debating, predicting, and communicating ideas to others. The list could go on and on.

Observations made by the teacher are essential if classroom assessment and evaluation are to be reliable and valid. In addition to being necessary for triangulating the evidence of learning, some learning can only be observed. Some students are better able to show what they know by doing it; these "in-action" learners may record little in writing and, therefore, will need some of their learning assessed through teacher observation. As products are constructed, teachers also have opportunities to observe students' learning *during* the learning, not just at the end of learning. When there isn't enough observational evidence, evaluations at reporting time are at risk of being invalid because they are not corroborated through multiple sources over time. (See Figures 1-16 and 1-17 for examples of observations in ELA and mathematics.)

Collecting Products

Teachers collect various kinds of evidence to show what students are able to do in relation to the standards or outcomes for the subject or grade level. These could include projects, assignments, notebooks, digital representations, and tests. There are many ways for students to represent their learning and if we, as teachers, prescribe the evidence of learning, we may unnecessarily limit students' options to show what they know. (See Figures 1-18 and 1-19 for different products that represent learning.)

▼ **Figure 1-18**

Possible Products as Evidence of Learning in Mathematical Problem-solving
• Work samples
• Math problems on tests
• Problem-based performance tasks

▼ **Figure 1-19**

Possible Products as Evidence of Learning in Language Arts (Digital and Paper-based)
• Reader response
• Writing folder
• Projects and assignments
• Reading log

Conversations About Learning

Conversations between teachers and students may be face-to-face, via recordings, online, or in written form (such as self-assessments, journal entries, or conferences). For example, teachers listen to learners during class meetings and during individual or group conferences. They also listen to recorded self-assessments or read students' self-assessments. Teachers also have opportunities to "listen" when students assess their work in relation to criteria, analyze work samples for their portfolios, or prepare to report to their parents about their learning.

As students think, do, and then explain, teachers listen and gather evidence about what they know and understand in relation to the standards or outcomes for the subject or grade level. Teachers then have better evidence to determine what students think about what they did or created; for example, students can talk about their best efforts, what was difficult or easy, what they might do differently next time, and what risks they have taken as learners. As students articulate their learning – as part of a reader's response, a mathematics response, or in some other way – they practice explaining their thinking. The ability to explain their thinking is helpful not only during the day-to-day moments in the classroom, but also during tests, performance tasks, or external assessments. This kind of intellectual engagement helps students become self-regulated learners – that is, students who are able to learn and take effective action both in and out of school. (See Figures 1-20 and 1-21 for examples of conversations in ELA and mathematics.)

**Possible Conversations as Evidence of
Learning in Language Arts**

- Literature circle records
- Partner reading criteria records
- Writing conference records
- Author's log kept by students
- Self-assessments by students
- Oral reading audio recordings with student self-assessments

**Possible Conversations as Evidence of
Learning in Mathematics**

- Conversations with students about their learning
- "Eavesdropping" on student conversations and small-group work
- Self-assessments in relation to criteria
- Do/Say/Write/Represent Math journal records
- Digital images of students at work
- Exit cards
- Whole-group discussions

Remember that we build reliability and validity when we pay attention to collecting evidence of student learning across an extended period of time and from a variety of sources. In essence, we really are triangulating – that is, we are taking information from three sources over time. (See Figure 1-22, which shows how product, observation, and conversation pull together from the perspective of mathematics. Each area repeats what has been highlighted in previous figures, but it is done this way in order to illustrate the complete body of evidence.)

In summary, teachers deliberately plan to collect a range of evidence – both qualitative and quantitative data – matching it to the curriculum standards for which they are responsible. They look at the learning destination and respond to some simple questions about both what will be collected and how it is going to be collected.

Different teachers collect different kinds of evidence of learning, even though the description of what their students need to learn may be the same. This is because the learning experiences that teachers design for different groups of learners may vary. Also, since students learn in different ways and at different rates, collections of evidence may vary in terms of how students choose to represent their learning.

Remember that all students need equal opportunities to show proof of learning regardless of how they learn, how they show their learning, or whether or not (or how much) they struggle.

The next step in developing an effective assessment plan is to collect some baseline evidence of learning.

Figure 1-22 ▼

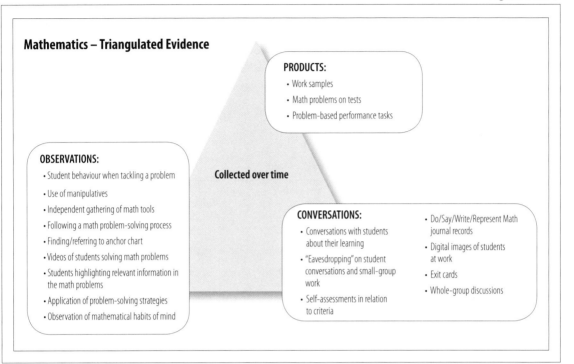

Mathematics – Triangulated Evidence

PRODUCTS:
- Work samples
- Math problems on tests
- Problem-based performance tasks

OBSERVATIONS:
- Student behaviour when tackling a problem
- Use of manipulatives
- Independent gathering of math tools
- Following a math problem-solving process
- Finding/referring to anchor chart
- Videos of students solving math problems
- Students highlighting relevant information in the math problems
- Application of problem-solving strategies
- Observation of mathematical habits of mind

Collected over time

CONVERSATIONS:
- Conversations with students about their learning
- "Eavesdropping" on student conversations and small-group work
- Self-assessments in relation to criteria
- Do/Say/Write/Represent Math journal records
- Digital images of students at work
- Exit cards
- Whole-group discussions

4. Collecting Baseline Evidence of Learning

As teachers collect products, conversations, and observations that provide evidence of students' learning, it is helpful for them to be able to demonstrate just how far students have progressed. That means early on, teachers need to collect evidence in critical areas so that the information gathered can later be used to compare student learning with their earliest levels of achievement. This type of evidence is often referred to as baseline evidence or baseline data. Because the term baseline is defined as "a minimum or starting point used for comparisons," collecting early evidence gives teachers a simple way to say: "You used to . . . and now you . . ." or for students themselves to say "I used to . . . and now I . . . ."

In this instance, teachers are paying close attention to and keeping track of how the students are performing early in their learning. At this point, the baseline data is not used for summative purposes but will be considered later on in the term in order to demonstrate how much the student has progressed. (See Figure 1-23 for an example of baseline evidence in ELA.)

▼ **Figure 1-23**

Baseline Evidence of Learning in ELA

Writing about self – letter to the teacher... I want to be a successful learner this year.
My strengths are:

The areas I need to improve are:

One goal I have for myself is:

In order to help me, you, as my teacher need to know...

Choose texts
- Favourite all time text
- Text currently reading
- Text I would like to read
- Read aloud. Record reading

Bring a sample of your writing you are most proud of and explain, in writing why you are proud of it. (Once students have brought in writing, analyze it or teach them to analyze it for specific skills and strategies to be taught during the term.)

Bring a research project you have from previous years.

Observations during group meetings, class time, small groups, and partner work (need a checklist to record data).

For example, a teacher in social studies may ask students to write a journal entry describing their reaction to a current event in their community. Additionally, students may be observed in small-group dialogue as they discuss the impact of that current event on their lives as students. The teacher can then identify patterns and trends across student performance and gain a clear idea about areas of strength and areas for instructional direction.

These two types of baseline evidence are critical as students will be responding in both written and oral form to current events and issues throughout the term. As the teacher reviews the student work and the data that was collected, the teacher's next instructional steps become clear. Later on in the term, the teacher might ask students to use the criteria that were subsequently constructed to compare their first written attempt to their growing understanding of the elements of an effective analysis and response to current community events. As students look back at previous work, they can make statements of progress backed up with evidence from their own work.

In summary, when teachers deliberately and consciously plan for the learning and reporting process, they prepare themselves to be responsive in their instructional and inquiry design. (See Appendix C for some planning questions that can support you as you respond to the opportunities that this chapter brings to your planning practice.)

The example found in Figure 1-24 provides a sample from social studies to illustrate the ways that teachers have used the planning questions to organize their thinking and action.

▼ **Figure 1-24**

Learning Destination

Learning Destination	Evidence of Learn	Samples/Models/Criteria
- I ask & answer questions about Canada and the world. - I will develop & practice skills in interpreting and creating maps. - I can find information from a variety of sources. - I can work cooperatively in a group situation. - I appreciate & value Canada's diversity. - I understand the passage of time. - I understand that people create systems of government. - I will develop the skills & attitudes necessary to become a thoughtful, active participant in my community and as a global citizen.	- checklist - oral presentation - debate - graphic organizer - build a diorama - make a timeline - write a play - role play - journal entry - write a song - written reports - posters - draw diagram - label map - build a model - interviews	- map - written report (all stages of writing process) - poster - journal entry - checklist - model (think aloud) use of graphic organizer - role model a debate - timeline

Now that you have planned to let your students and others, such as their parents, know what is expected of them, what the levels of quality are, the kinds of evidence that need to be produced, and the ways in which evidence will be collected, it is time to take action. In the next chapter – Activating and Engaging Learners – we describe in four easy steps just how you can do just that:

1. describing the learning destination and expected quality

2. involving students and providing time and support for them to learn

3. teaching to student needs based on assessment evidence

4. collecting reliable and valid evidence of learning

Activating and Engaging Learners Through Informative Assessment

"Assessment for learning is in place if students do not have to wait for the teacher to tell him or her what to do next. They know this themselves."

Mary Chamberlain

Classroom assessment has become a recognized field – separate from measurement and evaluation – over the past thirty years. It has developed in response to research by Crooks (1988) and Stiggins & Bridgeford (1985), as well as ongoing work by many educators and researchers, including those who meet periodically and regularly as part of the International Assessment Symposium.

Since the late 1980s, classroom assessment has been defined as:

- a set of methods and procedures grounded in research

- dependent upon teachers coming to understand the relevant standards/outcomes and agreed-upon statements of quality

- involving the collection of evidence of learning from multiple sources over time in relation to standards that is, potentially, as diverse as the students, teachers, and the various disciplines

- a learning process which engages students through assessment – examining samples, co-constructing criteria, self-assessing, collecting evidence of learning, and communicating learning to others

- dependent upon teachers' informed professional judgment, which, when evidence is collected from multiple sources over time, can be more reliable and valid than external test results

When teachers think about their most powerful teaching design, they are often referring to "assessment in the service of learning" strategies. There is a huge overlap between teaching excellence and the use of quality classroom assessment approaches. Being mindful of classroom assessment and grading and reporting *during* the learning makes sense for five reasons:

1. The primary purpose of assessment and evaluation is to support learning. Students who are engaged, motivated, and have a sense of ownership are more likely to learn.

2. The secondary purpose of assessment is to communicate and report that learning to others. Students who know what needs to be learned and students who understand quality can self-monitor their way to success, collect evidence of learning, and explain to others why the evidence is proof of learning; they can be partners in the classroom assessment process.

3. If teachers are to collect what they need for evidence of learning at the end of the learning time, they need to ensure its creation and collection *during* the learning. Having students involved in collecting evidence of learning in relation to learning goals means that it is increasingly likely that teachers will have more powerful and comprehensive collections of evidence of student learning.

4. Considering standards-based grading and reporting during learning makes sense also from a research perspective on learning (Crooks, 1988; Black & Wiliam, 1998; Looney, 2005), engagement (Stiggins, 2013), motivation (Butler, 1988; Covington, 1998; Harlen & Deakin Crick, 2002a, 2002b; Reay & Wiliam, 1999; Roderick & Engel, 2001) and reliability and validity of professional judgments (ARG, 2006; Burger et al., 2009; Gordon & Reese, 1997).

5. Classroom assessment is a research undertaking. Teachers must be present for the ongoing learning process in order to witness it. The result is that, by the end of the learning, teachers can say with confidence, "Look at the evidence. It is clear. This is what the student has learned."

Whether one refers to it as assessment *for* learning, assessment as learning, or assessment *in the service of* learning, formative assessment that includes the deep involvement of learners in the assessment process is a powerful instructional tool. In 1998, Black & Wiliam summarized their research findings by concluding that assessment for learning has the most powerful effect on student learning of any innovation *ever documented*. Research continues to support this finding. Teachers who want to have this kind of powerful effect use assessment *during* the learning to engage, motivate, and inspire students.

Consider the following nine actions that teachers can take to support, engage, and motivate learners in an environment of increased testing pressure. They are detailed in the

Assessment Reform Group's *Testing, Motivation, and Learning* (Harlen & Deakin Crick, 2002b, p. 8). The authors state that research shows that teachers need to "do more of this:"

1. Provide choice and help students to take responsibility for their learning.

2. Discuss with students the purpose of their learning and provide feedback that will help the learning process.

3. Encourage students to judge their work by how much they have learned and by the progress they have made.

4. Help students to understand the criteria by which their learning is assessed and to assess their own work.

5. Develop students' understanding of the goals of their work in terms of what they are learning; provide feedback to students in relation to these goals.

6. Help students to understand where they are in relation to learning goals and how to make further progress.

7. Give feedback that enables students to know the next steps and how to succeed in taking them.

8. Encourage students to value effort and a wide range of attainments.

9. Encourage collaboration among students, along with a positive view of each others' attainments.

Engagement in learning is directly connected to students' use of cognitive, meta-cognitive, and self-regulatory strategies that monitor and guide the learning process. When students are involved in the assessment process – examining samples, co-constructing criteria, self-assessing, collecting evidence of their learning, and communicating it to others – they are engaged in meaningful ways. In this chapter, we will describe what teachers need to *deliberately* and *intentionally* do in order to capitalize on the documented power of assessment to support student learning.

There are four classroom assessment functions that teachers can use in order to activate and engage even the youngest learners, during the learning:

1. describing the learning destination and expected levels of quality

2. involving students and providing time and support for them to learn

3. teaching to student needs based on assessment evidence

4. collecting reliable and valid evidence of learning

1. Describing the Learning Destination and Expected Levels of Quality

When teachers inform and involve students (and parents), when they know from the beginning what is needed in order to be successful, students learn more. Research highlights the importance of helping students picture quality and success. No wonder. Think about it. When teachers and students know where they are going, they are more likely to achieve success. Once students know what they are supposed to be learning, they can self-monitor, make adjustments, and learn more. That is why teachers talk about the learning destination in student-friendly language (see Figures 2-1 and 2-2), provide information about the relevance of the learning to their lives in and out of school, show samples and criteria to help learners understand quality and success, and identify potential evidence.

 Figure 2-1

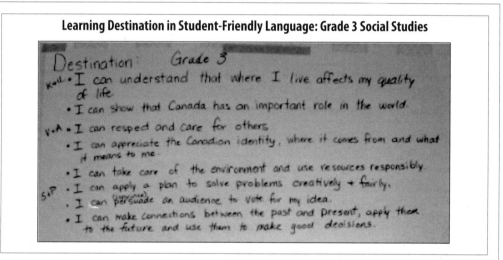

Learning Destination in Student-Friendly Language: Grade 3 Social Studies

Whether the standard has to do with writing, engaging in critical thinking, expressing new learning through a variety of representational formats, or applying an algorithm, the learning dictates the form of the evidence. For example, if the curriculum standard or learning outcome states that students should be able to "describe the difference between *homogeneous and heterogeneous*" there are multiple ways that they could show what they know. And, when they demonstrate what they know in different ways it doesn't mean the learning expectation has changed. How the student demonstrates progress towards that standard might be different from what others do; both, though, provide evidence of learning.

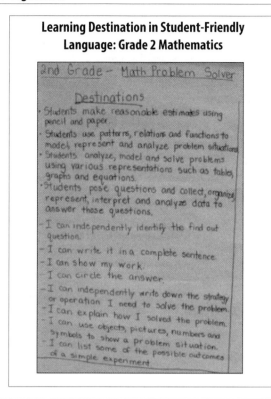

Learning Destination in Student-Friendly Language: Grade 2 Mathematics

Then, as teachers talk with students about what counts – evidence of learning – they share samples that illustrate a range of possibilities. They share or co-construct criteria for products, process, and collections of evidence so that the expected learning is explicit and learners can confirm, consolidate, and integrate new knowledge. In order to identify what quality and success can be, students look for what is common among the samples and the criteria. This process scaffolds future learning and helps teach about quality expectations. Also, the process of co-constructing criteria assists learners to understand and use the language of assessment to self-regulate and to self-monitor. (See Figures 2-3 and 2-4 for examples of co-constructed criteria.)

Figure 2-3 ▼

Grade 3, 4, 5 Multi-age Classroom: Co-constructing Criteria about *What counts when we write well?*

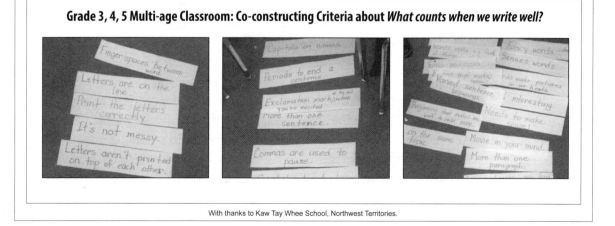

With thanks to Kaw Tay Whee School, Northwest Territories.

Criteria Co-constructed in a Grade 3 Classroom
What counts in solving a math problem?

Criteria	Details
Understand the problem	• Can tell all parts of the problem • Know what to do • Can tell if a part is missing
Choose a stragey to solve it	• Use diagrams to figure out • Think of similar problems that you have worked on • Try different ways until it works
Tell about how you reached the solution	• Break down the process into steps • Check work • Use mathematical language

Though we do not combine grades for achievement (in relation to outcomes) with grades for attitude, effort, work habits, or participation, we do know that there are habits of mind or learning skills that support students in their progress and growth. Teachers need to be just as clear about expectations for quality work habits or learning skills as they are for achievement in relation to outcomes, even though these may be reported to parents in a different section of the report card.

For example, a Grade 6-7-8 teacher wanted students to learn how to have a discussion. She arranged for three adults to come to her classroom. After introducing the adults and explaining that they were there to have a group discussion while the students analyzed what made an effective group discussion, the teacher wrote, "What counts… what matters… what is important when having a group discussion?" on the white board. Then she asked the adults to begin. After about two minutes, she stopped them and asked the students to talk to one another about what they had noticed. Once the ideas surfaced, she started to have students record them on sentence strips. She asked the adults to continue their discussion and stopped them again after another two minutes. The teacher repeated this process – adding more of the students' ideas to the collection of sentence strips. The teacher then asked the adults to have a non-productive discussion. The students were asked to observe. They noticed many behaviours that made a productive discussion impossible, such as talking over one another, name calling, and taking a cell phone call in the middle of the conversation. More ideas were added to the list. Then the students, under the direction of the teacher, grouped similar ideas together until all the strips had been sorted into three groups. Together, they decided the important criteria for a group discussion were: (See Figure 2-5.)

- Stay on topic and invite everyone to be involved.
- Listen and try to understand what others are saying/meaning.
- Contribute ideas that help the discussion move forward.

▼ **Figure 2-5**

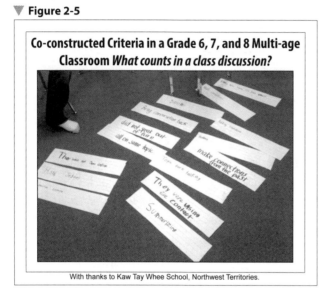

Co-constructed Criteria in a Grade 6, 7, and 8 Multi-age Classroom *What counts in a class discussion?*

With thanks to Kaw Tay Whee School, Northwest Territories.

Furthermore, this process helps students come to know and use the language of assessment, which then they and others (e.g., educational assistants, student support teachers, parents) can use to give specific, descriptive feedback during the learning. This is essential in order for students to self-monitor and self-regulate.

2. Involving Students and Providing Time and Support for Them to Learn

We can't just tell students what they need to learn and what their learning needs to look like. Just as teachers need to know what students know, are able to do, and can articulate, students also need to know for themselves what they know, are able to do, and can articulate. The strategies and structures that teachers use need to be simple, practical, and possible to use in busy classrooms. It is important for teachers to provide as much time as is possible, given reporting requirements and instructional time constraints, and for students to be involved, to give and receive specific and descriptive feedback, and to create and have a role in providing evidence of their learning.

Teachers seeking to involve students in classroom assessment engage students in:

- co-constructing criteria around process or products
- analyzing samples of student work
- undertaking self- and peer assessment in relation to criteria (feedback to self and others)
- setting meaningful goals
- collecting evidence of learning
- reflecting, selecting, and communicating proof of their learning to others

Some young students do seek feedback about how they are doing, but typically they do not seek evaluative feedback. However, students can quickly become used to receiving evaluative feedback – right, wrong, 65 percent, or 9/10. If students are used to evaluative feedback, they may need time to come to appreciate their role in the assessment process and learn how to self-monitor, self-assess, and self-regulate.

 Figure 2-6

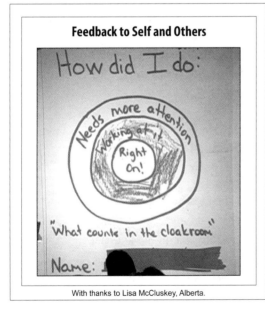

With thanks to Lisa McCluskey, Alberta.

For example, students learn to self-regulate and to self-monitor by using samples and co-constructed criteria. When teachers scaffold student self- and peer assessment in this way, both teachers and students see the power of assessment to support learning, to engage, and to motivate. These processes help students give themselves and others timely and specific feedback. (For some ideas, see Figure 2-6, Figure 2-7, and Figure 2-8.)

Self-assessment through a Math Journal

What I know about fractions

April 17   Fractions are 1/2 1/4 1/10 2/11 5/20ths

This is a fraction ➔

Pizza pieces are fractions

Fractions can be numbers or words like 1/2, one half,
3/8, three eighths

April 26   Adding up fractions is easy 1/2 + 1/3 and you can
subtract too.

1/2 is less than 1 - fractions aren't as big as real numbers.

Improper fractions have the top number
that is bigger 20/2

These are the same 1/2 = 2/4

May 5   Fractions can be mixed numbers like 3 1/2 or 1 2/5
and decimals are just like fractions because .5 = 1/2.

When you add or subtract, the bottom of the
fraction it has to be the same.

Change to 2/8 = 10/40
+2/10 = 8/40
Now add

May 5.
Please notice I
learned to +
and -
fractions. Now
I know they
are like
decimals.

© Gregory, Cameron & Davies (2011) *Self-Assessment and Goal Setting*, 2nd Edition, p. 35, Figure 13b.

▼ **Figure 2-8**

Solving Math Problems

Criteria	Details	Met	Not Yet Met
Understand the problem	• Can tell all parts of the problem • Know what to do • Can tell if a part is missing	√ √ √	
Choose a stragey to solve it	• Use diagrams to figure out	√	
	• Think of similar problems that you have worked on		√
	• Try different ways until it works	√	
Tell about how you reached the solution	• Break down the process into steps	√	
	• Check work		√
	• Use mathematical language	√	

Adapted from *Setting and Using Criteria* (2011) by Gregory, Cameron & Davies.

When we support students in giving themselves and others quality feedback, whether teachers are present or not, they have an opportunity to figure out what they know and what they need to learn next. They can take stock of where they are in relation to where they need to be if they are to be successful. This ensures that learners have the information they need to adjust so they can continually improve the quality of their work in relation to standards and more specific learning expectations. (See Figure 2-9, Figure 2-10, and Figure 2-11). In summary, when teachers deliberately share the purpose of self-assessment with their students, the students learn more.

▼ Figure 2-9

Grade 2 Learning to Self-assess in Relation to Criteria (Give Themselves Feedback)

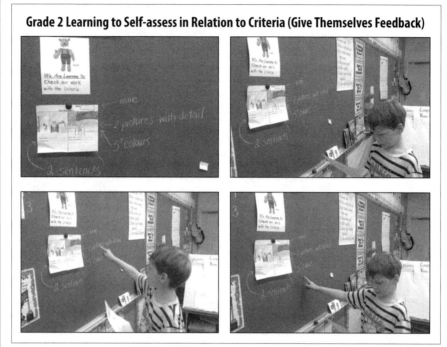

With thanks to Bridget Mawhinney, British Columbia.

▼ Figure 2-10

A student uses a sticky note to point out evidence that she had met her goal of adding more details to her diagram.

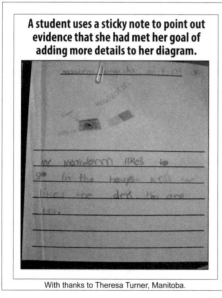

With thanks to Theresa Turner, Manitoba.

▼ Figure 2-11

Students made one comment in each area and then gave the criteria sheets back to their peers.

With thanks to Don Kusyk, Manitoba.

Setting specific, attainable goals is more possible when students have been engaged in co-constructing criteria for any product or process important to the class or the discipline. The goals identify the aspects of their work in relation to that co-constructed criteria that have not yet been met or do not yet match the samples or criteria. Through the use of samples and criteria, students make statements such as "I need to be able to pick out key information in word problems and decide which math operations make sense and why," instead of identifying broad goals like "I need to get better at math." (See Figure 2-12 for a transcript from a Grade 6 teacher talking about goals and Figure 2-13 for an example of students identifying a specific goal and then gathering evidence.)

▼ **Figure 2-12**

An Example of Specific Goals from Grade 6

My parent-student conferences focus on goal setting. Students share evidence with their parents to prove that they have worked on their goals. In order for that to happen at the end of each quarter, I need to start teaching goal setting from the very beginning of the school year. At first, I have students reflect on how they did in the Fifth Grade. What were their strengths and what were their challenges? Because of this, they can already set goals for the first quarter.

As I think back to when I first started asking my students to set goals, the goals that were identified were good. However, they would put them into their progress folios and that would essentially be it. We would not revisit those goals during class time until the end of the quarter. My students would then say things, such as, "Oh yah...that was my goal" but they had not intentionally worked on their goals and neither had I. It wasn't working. As a result, the process I use now is very different than before.

We still set goals from the very beginning of the year, but we now talk about what makes for a good writer, reader, mathematician, and so on. Therefore, students have specific language from which to draw in order to set their goals.

Instead of students creating a goal like "I want to be a better reader" they can draw upon the criteria that we have built to indicate an aspect of reading on which they need to focus. And, because of this specificity, students can more easily monitor and gather evidence of their progress towards their goals.

I also deliberately build time into our schedule so that they can look through their work. As a result, both my students and I are more confident in the area of goal setting and of communicating their growth.

Adapted from Noe Burnell, Hawai'i

Goal Envelope from a Grade 8/9 Class

Social Studies 8/9
Teacher: Ms Cyndi O'Rourke

Student Name: Brittney Brewer
Date: February 24? 0/05

Goal Envelope

My goal for this term is:

That I will hand my work in on time.

My evidence shows that I:

Am still working towards my goal

Have met my goal

Here are 3 pieces of evidence that prove this:

1. My one piece of evidence is showing that I am bla with unit 1.2 by a long shot.

2. I handed in my module project on time. ♡

3. I got 2.1 in on time (I think) but I'm still working on 2.2

With thanks to Cyndi O'Rourke, Yukon.

This process ensures that students receive specific and descriptive feedback from themselves, their peers, and their teachers. It gives students time to learn before receiving evaluative feedback. Then, based on the specific, descriptive feedback received, students can move their learning forward – that is, students, with their teachers' support, set goals and learn to adjust and refine their work in order to become more closely aligned with what is expected of them.

3. Teaching to Student Needs Based on Assessment Evidence

Feedback is important for students. But it is equally important for teachers, who are in a position to adjust their strategies to meet the needs or gaps in students' learning. Teachers use the process of formative assessment – some call it informative assessment – to guide their deliberate planning for each student's success. During this process, teachers determine what students know, can do, and can articulate. Next, they compare the learning with what students need to know. Then they deliberately plan ways to close the gap for each learner. This process is continuous, as teachers collect evidence of learning moment-by-moment in their classrooms. In order to engage in formative assessment successfully, teachers:

- routinely collect and use baseline data in relation to key concepts and processes prior to planning for learning and implementing the instructional sequence.

- assess what students know, are able to do, and can articulate during the instruction, based on the evidence of what has been learned and what has not yet been learned.

Teachers accomplish the steps in this process in various ways, depending on the subject and grade level in which they are working and on their own personal preferences. For example, many teachers collect evidence of student learning and progress at the beginning of the year and prior to the end of each term. They also collect evidence along the way. The baseline evidence that has been gathered helps to prove, in an authentic manner, how a student's work and learning has improved; it identifies instructional pathways, helps motivate students as they see their progress, and is a powerful way to help parents understand the learning journey for their child. As teachers consider the evidence at these critical times, they come to better understand patterns and trends in student learning and achievement. This, in turn, helps them plan instruction. Teachers can target what instructional next steps need to be taken for the group, as well as for specific sub-groups or individuals; they also know which groups of students may require additional support.

Consider these examples:

Example 1: *A Grade 7 mathematics teacher has students use small personal whiteboards. As he provides students with instruction in a particular concept, he has students work through an algorithm or problem on the whiteboard. He walks around the classroom looking over the students' shoulders to notice what they are doing well and where they are struggling. He then returns to the front of the classroom and carries on with instruction that tightly fits the needs of the students at that very moment.*

Example 2: *One teacher co-constructed criteria with her primary students about "What's important when we are working in partners?" When it is time to actually work in pairs, students review the list of criteria and the teacher asks two students to take the clipboards and be "Process Observers" during partner time. The process observers have a sheet with the criteria and a place to take notes about what they notice students doing to prove that they know how to be good learning partners.*

Example 3: *Teachers identify the learning goals and objectives for the week's instructional design. Then, as they observe students during the day, they highlight students' names in the following way:*

- *highlighted in green – they've got it.*
- *highlighted in orange – they've nearly got it*
- *highlighted in red – they've not got it at all*

At the end of the week, they look at each child's learning to determine next week's plan, including whether they need to take a step back or move forward.

Example 4: *A science teacher has shared the criteria that specifically describes what safety looks like in his lab. As he observes the students, he writes down the initials of the students who are meeting the criteria and those who are not yet meeting them. At the beginning of the next class period, he gathers the students whom he had noted were not yet meeting some of the required criteria and does a quick mini-lesson highlighting the safe use of the equipment.*

Example 5: *A Grade 3 teacher has noticed that many of her students are struggling to compose beginnings to their writing that capture the reader's attention and provide evidence of the criteria that was established as the class considered a wide variety of story openings. Her next mini-lesson focuses on this. She reviews the criteria with the students and shares a picture prompt with them. She asks the students what they see in the picture prompt and jots those ideas down on chart paper. The class challenges her to write a start to a story, based on the image, using the information that they have provided, while being mindful of the criteria. She writes the story beginning in front of them, saying aloud what is going on in her mind as she is writing. Once finished, she reviews the story opening and highlights where in the writing the criteria is present. (See Figure 2-14.)*

▼ **Figure 2-14**

Grade 3 Teacher - Criteria

With thanks to Susanna Nigro-Vecchio, Alberta.

The next part of working with students during the learning is to have them collect the evidence of what they know, what they are able to do, and what they can articulate.

4. Collecting Reliable and Valid Evidence of Learning

There are endless ways for both teachers and students to collect triangulated evidence of learning. It is important that teachers find the ways that suit them. Here are several examples that teachers find useful:

Example 1: *A Grade 2 teacher has her students use manipulatives to solve mathematical problems. Because students will use manipulatives throughout the entire school year, they have co-constructed criteria about the appropriate use of manipulatives to solve math problems. The criteria are (the teacher language is in the brackets):*

- *I choose manipulatives that make sense to solve the math problem. (selection–S)*
- *I use the manipulatives in a safe way. (appropriate use–U)*
- *The manipulatives leave a trail of my math thinking on my table top. (solve in a logical way–L)*
- *I can write using words or numbers or symbols what the manipulatives are telling me about the math problem. (transcribe manipulatives into symbols–T)*

The teacher set up an observational checklist with these ideas. See Figure 2-15 for a sample. As she observes the students using their manipulatives, the teacher circles the letters that represent what the students are demonstrating during that class period. Though she observes all of her students throughout the class, her goal is to record her observations for about four or five students each time. This strategy allows her observations to last past the event, without the need to scribe and document each word or student action.

Recording Observations in a Mathematics Class

Names	Date 9/12	Date 9/25	Date	Date	Date
Kailey	SULT	SULT	SULT	SULT	SULT
Jeremy	SULT	SULT	SULT	SULT	SULT
Maya	SULT	SULT	SULT	SULT	SULT
Lucca	SULT	SULT	SULT	SULT	SULT
Nicholas	SULT	SULT	SULT	SULT	SULT
Annie	SULT	SULT	SULT	SULT	SULT
Ashley	SULT	SULT	SULT	SULT	SULT
Clarence	SULT	SULT	SULT	SULT	SULT
Harriet	SULT	SULT	SULT	SULT	SULT
Najoua	SULT	SULT	SULT	SULT	SULT
Marie-Cecile	SULT	SULT	SULT	SULT	SULT
Tarah	SULT	SULT	SULT	SULT	SULT
Pierre	SULT	SULT	SULT	SULT	SULT
Angela	SULT	SULT	SULT	SULT	SULT

Acronym: SULT
S for Selection
U for appropriate Use
L for solve in Logical way
T for Transcribe manipulatives into symbols

Example 2: *A Grade 6 teacher in a social studies class invited his students to present evidence of their learning in five areas: strength, improvement, successful collaboration, originality, and an area of student choice. Students looked through their work to identify a product, observation, or conversation that, for them, would best represent each of these five areas. The students then presented the evidence to their teacher and, as they talked through the choices, the teacher made notes to represent the conversation and to add to each student's collection of evidence. (See Figure 2-16.)*

Figure 2-16 ▼

Example 3: *A Grade 6 teacher identified competencies that touch each subject area. They are:*

- *I can manage information.*
- *I am a clear and effective communicator.*
- *I know how to learn.*
- *I am a creative and practical problem-solver.*

Students collect evidence across subject areas that provide evidence that they can manage information, can communicate clearly and effectively, know how to learn, and are able to solve problems creatively and practically. About every three weeks, students are provided with time to look through their work to add to their portfolio. A proof card that describes what the sample is providing evidence of accompanies each selection. (See Figure 2-17.)

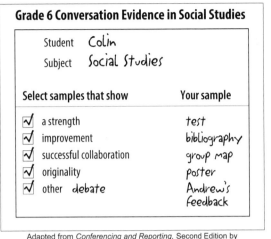

Grade 6 Conversation Evidence in Social Studies

Student   Colin

Subject   Social Studies

Select samples that show	Your sample
☑ a strength	test
☑ improvement	bibliography
☑ successful collaboration	group map
☑ originality	poster
☑ other debate	Andrew's feedback

Adapted from *Conferencing and Reporting*, Second Edition by Gregory, Cameron & Davies, p.19, Figure 2.

Teachers understand that their professional judgments of students' achievement are dependent on collecting evidence that is both reliable and valid. They deliberately plan to collect that evidence from observations, conversations, and products. They do not do this alone. Though teachers observe students both in process and in conversation and make notes that can be collated or considered, the student is also actively involved in the process of evidence collection.

▼ **Figure 2-17**

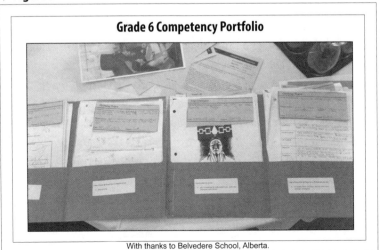

Grade 6 Competency Portfolio

With thanks to Belvedere School, Alberta.

As learners self-assess and reflect, and as they create, write, draw, and use symbols, they produce evidence that can be selected for placement in a portfolio or can be provided to the teacher for feedback, assessment, and evaluation. This is a joint process and does not rest solely with the teacher or the learner.

It is the student who determines the work that best shows her competencies in these areas. Selection is an active process and, during the process of putting the portfolio together, students come to more deeply understand the work. Students' conversations with self (that is, reflecting on their ability to listen, express views and perspectives, and on journal entries that document the stages of work towards the end-of-semester project) might also be considered as evidence.

Social media have expanded the possibilities for extending our community by changing the way we communicate and stay in touch. Communication can still be print-based, but, more and more often, the possibilities include such methods as emails; class or student blogs; interaction in online communities; twitter tweets; work samples (digital or paper-based); presentations (in person or online, in school or at home); and files and portfolios (digital or paper-based) containing collections of evidence.

Teachers are reminded that every subject area has a communication thread that is unique to the discipline. Communicating with others in ways appropriate to the discipline not only gives students practice (while also giving teachers evidence), but provides an audience for the communication. Secondly, since the people doing the work are learning the most, students need to be doing most of the communicating.

Here are three examples that highlight ways that students are communicating what they are learning.

Example 1: *A Grade 7 teacher teaches his students how to use the Aurasma application. Students select three pieces of work that they believe best demonstrate their understanding of the scientific content and processes studied this term. For each piece of work, a fellow student, using the classroom handheld device, takes a video of the student referring to the work as she talks about why it provides the best evidence of what has been uncovered and learned. Using the Aurasma application, the students then pair each video clip with the actual piece of student work. When it is time to consider this collection of evidence of learning, the teacher positions the classroom handheld device over the piece of student work and the video of the student talking about that very same work is activated and plays. In this way, both the product and the conversation are captured and can be revisited over and over again.*

Example 2: *A Grade 1 teacher takes pictures of students' completed manipulative work with the classroom handheld device. Students upload the photograph into an application such as Educreations, ShowMe, or Explain Everything. They record themselves talking about their mathematical thinking and also annotate the picture by drawing on it to better describe their thinking. The teacher does not need to scribe what the student said, but rather this recording exists after the conversation with either the teacher or another student has ended. It can be accessed at any time. (See Figure 2-18.)*

Example 3: *A Grade 4 teacher pulls individual students aside while they are inquiring into the question that the class posed: "Why are streams still called fresh water when they are polluted?" Using the Quick Voice Pro application, the teacher poses a question to the student. For example, "What do you know now about our question that you did not know before?" or "What other questions are you thinking about as you research?" or "What would you tell someone else about what you are learning?" This student response is recorded using the application and then emailed to the child's parents, as well as the teacher. The recording is a conversation that serves as a piece of evidence of that child's learning and development.*

▼ **Figure 2-18**

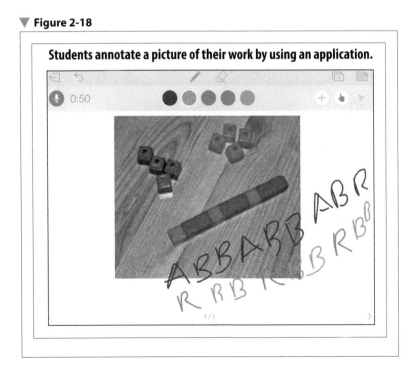

Students annotate a picture of their work by using an application.

As teachers ask students to provide evidence of learning in the ways described above, they have them select the proof of learning in relation to the standards-based learning goals for the subject – the student-friendly learning destination shared with students early in the course. Because the teacher has planned for a variety of triangulated evidence, this process helps students come to understand that success has many different looks; evidence of what one has learned can be shown in a variety of ways. Additionally, students also come to understand that they have a responsibility to show proof of learning. Teachers also need to collect evidence of student learning, and they must help students to become involved in communicating that learning to others.

In summary, we give students time to learn and time to "get it right" by helping them understand the learning destination, by co-constructing criteria around process or products, and by involving them in analyzing samples of student work. Then, as they create evidence of learning, teachers engage students in self- and peer assessment and goal setting in relation to the criteria that they have helped to construct. As the learning proceeds, teachers ask students to collect specific evidence of learning in relation to the learning goals; students are supported in reviewing the evidence they have collected, in selecting proof of their learning, and in reflecting on that proof. Lastly, they communicate their evidence of learning to others.

Now that students are engaged, motivated, learning, collecting evidence of learning alongside teachers, and communicating their learning to others, it is time for teachers to plan the summative assessment: the evaluation process. In the next chapter – After the Learning – we will help you do just that in four easy steps:

1. finalizing the collection of evidence of learning (including the role of formative and summative assessment evidence)

2. making informed professional judgments

3. reporting learning and achievement using required format (percentages, letter grades, number grades, or other symbols)

4. involving students in the reporting process

After the Learning: Evaluating and Reporting to Others

"Summative assessment by teachers is the process by which teachers gather evidence in a planned and systematic way in order to draw inferences about their students' learning, based on their professional judgment, and to report at a particular time on their students' achievements."
Assessment Reform Group (2006, p. 4)

"Evaluation and reporting occur at the point in the classroom assessment cycle when the learning pauses, and the evidence is organized and evaluated by comparing it to what students needed to learn. Then, the results of the evaluation are shared through the reporting process" (Davies, 2011, p. 93). When teachers approach reporting time having begun with the end in mind, having thought through evidence of learning and having involved students in the assessment process, including evidence of learning, stress is significantly diminished. The hard work of teaching and learning is almost done. The evidence collections are complete. Students have shared their perspectives on what they have learned. Teachers are now ready to make their professional judgments and then report.

As they do these last tasks, teachers review the evidence that they have collected. Some teachers choose to compile and collate it. Others do not. What all teachers do, though, is make decisions about which evidence best shows what students now know, understand, can do, and articulate in relation to those standards and expectations that have guided the teaching and learning to this point.

Once the evidence of learning has been reviewed, teachers compare that evidence to the level of quality that is expected and make informed professional judgments that have been developed through ongoing work with colleagues. Then, teachers communicate their professional judgment using the report card and its required format – symbols, narrative, a combination, or something else entirely. Lastly, teachers arrange to have students show evidence of their learning to parents either at home, at school, or online. That's it! Done! And done well!

Now, let's review this process step-by-step so that you can make your own plans. *After* the learning, and as you move on to evaluating and reporting, there are four tasks:

1. finalizing the collection of evidence of learning
2. making informed professional judgments
3. reporting learning and achievement using required format (percentages, letter grades, number grades, or other symbols)
4. involving students in the reporting and informing process

1. Finalizing the Collection of Evidence of Learning

After the learning, students and teachers revisit, for the last time, their collections of evidence in relation to the student-friendly learning destination. Teachers ask students to look for the best proof that they have met *all* the learning standards or outcomes in a subject area. This looks a little different in an early primary class than in a class with older students, but the process is the same. Since everything that a student says, does, or creates is potential evidence, this is the time for students to work in partnership with their teacher to select and present their best evidence in relation to the learning destination.

In the following accounts, students and teachers work together to gather a final body of evidence.

Example 1: *Grade 5 teacher, Ms. N, creates a series of "proof cards" (Gregory, Cameron & Davies, 2011) in mathematics. They include cards with the headers: "My best math response…," "Proof that I can solve complex problems…," "I used mathematical vocabulary here…," "I made a connection between math and another subject area when I…," etc. Students review their work to find the best evidence to match the proof cards' descriptors. The proof cards, with a brief reflection, are attached to each piece of work and are inserted into a file folder for Ms. N to use later as she is making summative decisions. (See Figure 3-1.)*

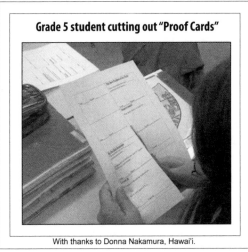

▼ **Figure 3-1**

Grade 5 student cutting out "Proof Cards"

With thanks to Donna Nakamura, Hawai'i.

Figure 3-2 ▼

Example 2: *During numeracy centre time, Ms. C meets with small groups of four Grade 1 students at a time to sort their math work into three groups for the term – graphing, shapes, and numbers. She works with the students to select one piece from each of the three groups that would illustrate something that they now know more about than when they started. She speaks to them about what specifically it is that they learned. Once they are able to articulate that understanding, the students write it down in a frame that will accompany each piece of work in their portfolio. (See Figure 3-2.)*

Teacher and student talking about evidence.

With thanks to Allison Carveiro, Hawai'i.

Figure 3-3 ▼

Student:		OEN:	Grade:	Homeroom:

Learning Skills and Work Habits

E – Excellent   G – Good   S – Satisfactory   N – Needs Improvement

Responsibility	Organization
• Fulfils responsibilities and commitments within the learning environment. • Completes and submits class work, homework, and assignments according to agreed-upon timelines. • Takes responsibility for and manages own behaviour.	• Devises and follows a plan and process for completing work and tasks. • Establishes priorities and manages time to complete tasks and achieve goals. • Identifies, gathers, evaluates, and uses information, technology, and resources to complete tasks.
Independent Work	**Collaboration**
• Independently monitors, assesses, and revises plans to complete tasks and meet goals. • Uses class time appropriately to complete tasks. • Follows instructions with minimal supervision.	• Accepts various roles and an equitable share of work in a group. • Responds positively to the ideas, opinions, values, and traditions of others. • Builds healthy peer-to-peer relationships through personal and media-assisted interactions. • Works with others to resolve conflicts and build consensus to achieve group goals. • Shares information, resources, and expertise, and promotes critical thinking to solve problems and make decisions.
Initiative	**Self-Regulation**
• Looks for and acts on new ideas and opportunities for learning. • Demonstrates the capacity for innovation and a willingness to take risks. • Demonstrates curiosity and interest in learning. • Approaches new tasks with a positive attitude. • Recognizes and advocates appropriately for the rights of self and others.	• Sets own individual goals and monitors progress towards achieving them. • Seeks clarification or assistance when needed. • Assesses and reflects critically on own strengths, needs, and interests. • Identifies learning opportunities, choices, and strategies to meet personal needs and achieve goals.

Adapted from Ministry of Education-Ontario (2010) *Growing Success: Assessment, Evaluation, and Reporting in Ontario Schools.*

Example 3: *In Mr. P's Grade 8 social studies class, students are asked to reflect on their learning at the end of each term in relation to three of the five learning skills on their report cards. (See Figure 3-3 for the Learning Skills.) Students select a piece of work that proves that they have demonstrated these learning skills during the last three months of instruction. Using an application, such as Aurasma, students take a video of themselves talking about why that particular piece of work is good evidence to show that they have exhibited the learning skill. Once the video and an image of the work is paired, Mr. P can review the students' reflections and use it as he makes his summative decisions. (See Figure 3-3a.)*

▼ **Figure 3-3a**

Using Aurasma to view a student talking about his work.

With thanks to K'alemi Dene School, Northwest Territories.

Teachers review the evidence of learning that students have collected and the evidence that they themselves have collected over time. This includes observations, conversations, and products, which may be in numeric or qualitative form. As teachers examine the evidence, they consider "best evidence" in terms of validity and reliability. This outcomes- or standards-based grading and reporting process honours teachers' informed professional judgment and provides a way for teachers to support students as they take a variety of learning pathways to success and quality. It is both fair and equitable.

Once there is a collection of evidence to represent the students' learning, it is time for teachers to make an informed professional judgment.

2. Making Informed Professional Judgments

Evaluating and reporting are less stressful and can be done with confidence when they are the last steps in a purposeful, systematic, multi-step process that does not come into play simply at the end of learning. Rather, it begins when teachers come to understand the standards or learning outcomes and the appropriate quality levels expected for a particular subject or grade level. Evaluating and reporting are further informed when teachers meet with others to come to a common understanding of quality and expectations. Then, once the evidence of learning has been collected from multiple sources over time, teachers begin a process of examining the evidence – both qualitative and quantitative – and make a decision regarding whether and to what degree students know, understand, can apply, and can articulate what is detailed by the standards or learning outcomes.

Evaluating and reporting require professional judgment in the context of the following four questions:

1. What does the student know, what is she or he able to do, and what can she or he articulate?

2. How is the student progressing in relation to the expectations for students in a similar age range, given curricular and standards documents?

3. What areas require further attention or development? What areas are of particular strength?

4. In what ways can the student's further learning be supported?

Professional judgment becomes more informed with reflection, practice, and ongoing collegial conversations that involve looking at student work from classrooms that are using protocols and examining student data generated from a variety of sources. (See Figure 3-4.) The protocol that colleagues used at an earlier stage to come to a common understanding of quality can be used again during and after the learning to check and affirm that the earlier views of quality are still commonly held.

As mentioned earlier, informed professional judgment results from teaching to the standards or learning outcomes based on a common reporting scale (often decided by the jurisdiction); it is also based on thoughtfully considering samples of student work and collections of evidence, scoring common assessments, and analyzing external test data with colleagues. While a teacher's written and verbal comments may speak to the amount of *growth* students have made in their learning, the evaluation must reflect their *progress* in relation to the standards for the subject area or course and the grade level at which they are working.

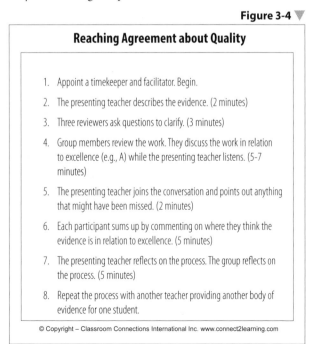

Figure 3-4 ▼

Reaching Agreement about Quality

1. Appoint a timekeeper and facilitator. Begin.

2. The presenting teacher describes the evidence. (2 minutes)

3. Three reviewers ask questions to clarify. (3 minutes)

4. Group members review the work. They discuss the work in relation to excellence (e.g., A) while the presenting teacher listens. (5-7 minutes)

5. The presenting teacher joins the conversation and points out anything that might have been missed. (2 minutes)

6. Each participant sums up by commenting on where they think the evidence is in relation to excellence. (5 minutes)

7. The presenting teacher reflects on the process. The group reflects on the process. (5 minutes)

8. Repeat the process with another teacher providing another body of evidence for one student.

We have said numerous times in this text (and deliberately repeat now), *everything* a student says, does, or creates is potentially evidence of learning. It is important that teachers use the evidence available for each student and compare it to the standards or learning outcomes that students are expected to achieve. In a standards-based evaluation system, teachers have to account for each student's learning in relation to the expectations for that grade and subject area and, we stress, not compare his or her work to the work of other students in the class. Furthermore, if an assignment has been missed or shown to be incomplete, that does not automatically mean that no evidence exists. Because evidence has been gathered from multiple sources over time, information from other pieces of evidence (products, observations, or conversations) may, in fact, demonstrate proof of the learning outcome, expectation, or standard.

While teachers do not have to base their evaluative decision on the same body of evidence of learning for each student, they must base their evaluation on a reliable and valid collection of evidence of learning. And this evaluation must be equitable – that is, all students, regardless of how they learn, show their learning, or how much they struggle (or not), must have the same opportunities to show proof of learning. A helpful definition of the term *informed professional judgment* is: the professional determination, after a review of evidence of learning present (not absent), of what has been learned and achieved.

We need to stress that using a mathematical algorithm such as adding the scores and averaging them misrepresents the learning that has been accomplished. To evaluate well, we should look at *all* the evidence: observations, products, and conversations. *Triangulation of evidence* is essential because it puts single pieces of evidence into context. Just as a judge in a court of law must examine all the evidence in light of the legal statutes, teachers must look at all the evidence in light of the description of learning based on the standards or learning outcomes. They must consider the entire range of information (all the quantitative and qualitative data): the proof students have collected, the self-assessments they have made, teacher observations, criteria-based assessments attached to projects or assignments, and the evidence that teachers have collected, including performance grids, rubric scores, and grades from projects and tests. As teachers examine all the evidence, they are seeking to make the most informed and defensible final professional judgment possible.

It is at this point that many of the "hot issues" currently being debated about reporting cease to matter. For example, whether the evidence of learning was produced in the midst of learning time (formative) or at the end of learning time (summative) isn't an issue. The timing is just information for the teacher. The Assessment Reform Group (2006, p. 10) states: "For summative purposes, common criteria need to be applied and achievement is summarized in terms of levels or grades, which must have the same meaning for all pupils. This means that if the information already gathered and used formatively is to be used for summative assessment it must be reviewed against the broader criteria that define reporting levels or grades. Change over time can be taken into account so that preference is given to the best evidence that shows the pupil's achievement across a range of work during the period covered by the summative assessment." Further, if that evidence was turned in late, or the work was incomplete, or if it was submitted after six feedback cycles with the teacher, it is, once again, simply information about the evidence itself.

Figure 3-5 ▼

Reporting Guidelines – Checking for Alignment and Consistency

Agreement about Quality

The Learning Destination (in relation to Standards or Outcomes)

1. Are report card grades given for the full range of educational standards or outcomes, not just those easiest to measure?

2. Has evidence of learning been selected because of its alignment with outcomes and standards?

Reliable and Valid Evidence of Learning

3. Are the report card grades based upon a wide array of evidence from multiple sources over time so as to ensure validity and reliability?

4. Do students understand expectations and acceptable evidence?

5. Are students involved in co-constructing criteria in relation to products, processes, and collections of evidence of learning?

6. Does the summative evaluation take place after students have time and opportunity to learn?

Evaluation at the End of Learning in Preparation for Reporting

7. Are report card grades derived from evidence present, not absent (thus devoid of practices such as assigning zeros or penalty deductions as a default stance, grading on a curve, averaging)?

8. Are report card grades for achievement of standards or learning outcomes reported separately from other non-achievement factors such as effort, attitude, attendance, and punctuality?

9. Are the report card grades reflective of a student's most consistent, more recent pattern of performance in relation to course learning goals based on the relevant standards and outcomes, as well as pre-determined levels of quality?

Informed Professional Judgment

10. Do report card grades reflect informed teacher professional judgment of the level of quality of student work in relation to the standards or outcomes?

11. Are report card grades validated by and anchored in collaborative conversation and analysis of student work against agreed-upon criteria by teachers across grade levels and subjects?

12. Are report card grades reflective of and illustrated by collections of exemplars and samples that illustrate levels of quality and achievement?

© 2012 Davies, Herbst, and Parrott Reynolds. *Transforming Schools and Systems Using Assessment: A Practical Guide.* (pp.103-104).

In summary, we state emphatically that what matters is that the final evaluation *must* represent students' actual learning and achievement in relation to the standards or learning outcomes for the course. Many jurisdictions have clearly identified guidelines to support and clearly communicate the principles that serve as a foundation to the act of reporting. (See Figure 3-5 which is adapted from *Transforming Schools and Systems Using Assessment: A Practical Guide* (2012) by Davies, Herbst & Parrott Reynolds.)

3. Reporting Learning and Achievement Using Required Format

Once teachers have exercised their professional judgment, and once that final judgment has been made, they represent their decision using a percentage, letter grade, number grade, symbol, rubric score, narrative, or other symbol – whatever form is required by policy and regulation. In order to finalize the report, teachers summarize students' strengths and areas needing improvement, and students and parents review the evidence. We use the term *reporting process* because reporting is not merely an event that produces a product – that is, the report card – but rather, it is a process that includes the work before teachers meet with students, during the learning time, and at the end.

The following examples are accounts from teachers who were required to report using a variety of symbols and reporting structures. As you read, reflect on what you can learn from them. Consider what is similar to your own reporting process and what is different. Ask yourself, "Is there anything in this account that can help improve my reporting process?"

▼ **Figure 3-6**

Description of Math proficiency for a term	
Criteria	**Details**
I can use numbers to solve problems	• Add multi digits • Add single digits • Subtract multi digits • Subtract single digits • Represent relationships between 1, 10, 100, 1000 • Explain relationships between 1, 10, 100, 1000 • Estimate length, height, depth, perimeter • Record length, height, depth, perimeter
I can use mathematical language	• Cm, mm, dm, m, km, perimeter, measure, predict, record, ones, tens, hundreds, thousands • Reflect on mathematical understanding • Make mathematical conjectures • Help other understand mathematical thinking
I can think like a mathematician	• Make connections • Represent mathematical ideas • Order standard units of measurement • Compare standard units of measurement • Draw items using a ruler • Estimate to judge reasonableness • Understand problems • Make a plan • Implement a plan • Look back • Select appropriate learning tools • Select appropriate computational strategies • Justify results

Example 1: *Mrs. D is required to report using percentages. She has defined what it means to be a successful student in mathematics and shared this with the students and parents. (See Figure 3-6.) Mrs. D collects evidence of learning and students also collect evidence of learning. At the end of the term, Mrs. D reviews the student work that has been collected in three areas:*

- *I can use numbers to solve problems.*
- *I can use mathematical language.*
- *I can think like a mathematician.*

The scoring guide shared with the students defines quality and proficiency in these areas and is attributed to 60 percent of the final grade. The remaining 40 percent is based on observations and interview notes, as well as quantitative data that Mrs. D has collected over the term from assignments, projects, and tests.

Example 2: *Mr. H is required to report using letter grades. Rather than using a numerical spread to represent quality at each level, Mr. H worked with his Grade 3 colleagues and defined each letter grade in terms of the quality of evidence that would be required to be present. In this way, the letter grade better aligns with the standards or learning outcomes for which he is responsible. (See Figure 3-7.)*

Figure 3-7 ▼

Description of an "A"

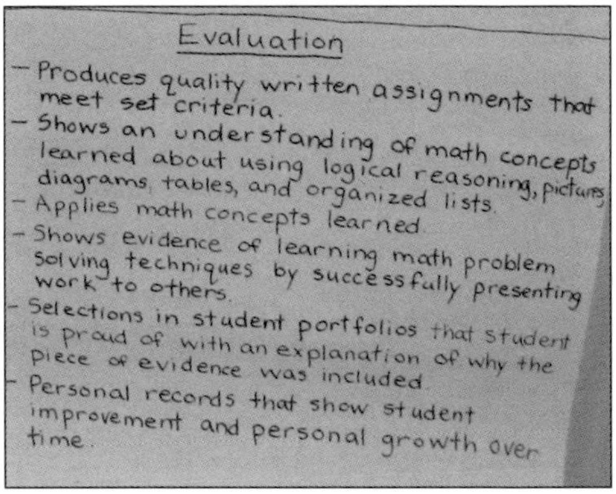

Evaluation
- Produces quality written assignments that meet set criteria.
- Shows an understanding of math concepts learned about using logical reasoning, pictures, diagrams, tables, and organized lists
- Applies math concepts learned.
- Shows evidence of learning math problem solving techniques by successfully presenting work to others
- Selections in student portfolios that student is proud of with an explanation of why the piece of evidence was included
- Personal records that show student improvement and personal growth over time.

▼ **Figure 3-8**

What Does Quality Look Like at Grade 3 in Reading?

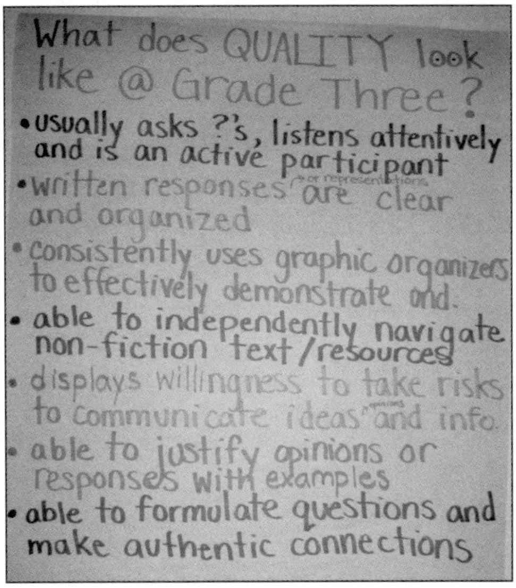

What does QUALITY look like @ Grade Three?
- usually asks ?'s, listens attentively and is an active participant
- written responses or representations are clear and organized
- consistently uses graphic organizers to effectively demonstrate and.
- able to independently navigate non-fiction text/resources
- displays willingness to take risks to communicate ideas and info
- able to justify opinions or responses with examples
- able to formulate questions and make authentic connections

Example 3: *In a school that has elected to move towards level descriptors (4, 3, 2, 1), Ms. M prepares for reporting student learning by comparing written descriptions of what a high-quality performance would look like for each standard. The description of "What does quality look like at Grade 3?" makes it clear to herself and to her students what was expected in ELA this term in order to receive a "4" on the report card. (See Figure 3-8.)*

▼ Figure 3-9

Description of Scientific Method – Proficient

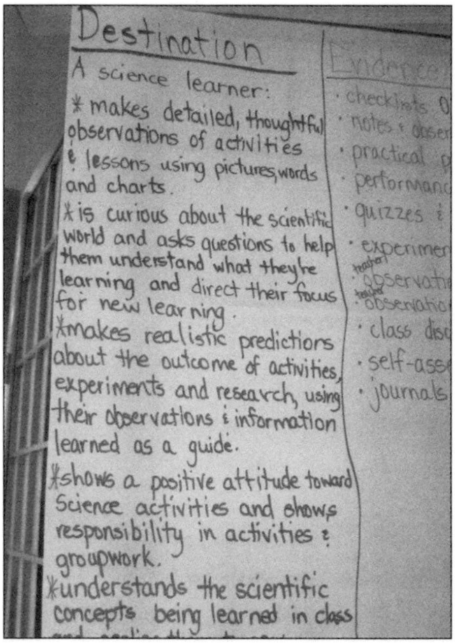

Destination

A science learner:
* makes detailed, thoughtful observations of activities & lessons using pictures, words and charts.
* is curious about the scientific world and asks questions to help them understand what they're learning and direct their focus for new learning.
* makes realistic predictions about the outcome of activities, experiments and research, using their observations & information learned as a guide.
* shows a positive attitude toward Science activities and shows responsibility in activities & groupwork.
* understands the scientific concepts being learned in class

Evidence
• checklists o
• notes & obser
• practical p
• performanc
• quizzes &
• experimen
• observatio
• observatio
• class disc
• self-asses
• journals

Example 4: *An intermediate teacher examined all the required outcomes in science and divided them into two categories: the scientific method and scientific concepts. He then detailed what was important for students to know, do, and be able to articulate about the scientific method. (See Figure 3-9.) As he planned the instructional sequences for his students, he identified the products, performance tasks, assignments, quizzes, and tests that he wanted to collect. In addition, he described what he would see and hear if students were engaged in the scientific process. This became his observation guide. (See Figure 3-9a.) He also explained the scientific method using three categories: beginning, on-the-way, and proficient. The students' final report card scores were based on their more recent evidence of learning in terms of the scientific method, along with evidence regarding content understanding.*

▼ Figure 3-9a

Recording Observations in a Science Class

Names	Date 9/12	Date 9/25	Date	Date	Date
Therese	ⓋMACD	ⓋⓂACD	VMACD	VMACD	VMACD
Kahele	ⓋMACD	ⓋⓂACD	VMACD	VMACD	VMACD
Giselle	ⓋⓂACD	ⓋⓂACD	VMACD	VMACD	VMACD
Mario	VⓂACD	ⓋⓂAⒸD	VMACD	VMACD	VMACD
Merissa	VⓂACD	ⓋⓂACD	VMACD	VMACD	VMACD
Jhameel	ⓋⓂAⒸD	ⓋⓂAⒸD	VMACD	VMACD	VMACD
Kevin	ⓋMACD	ⓋⓂACD	VMACD	VMACD	VMACD
André	ⓋⓂACD	ⓋⓂAⒸD	VMACD	VMACD	VMACD
Liana	ⓋⓂACD	ⓋⓂACD	VMACD	VMACD	VMACD
Stacey	VⓂAⒸD	VⓂAⒸD	VMACD	VMACD	VMACD
Yvan	ⓋⓂAⒸD	ⓋⓂAⒸD	VMACD	VMACD	VMACD
Waianela	ⓋⓂAⒸD	ⓋⓂACD	VMACD	VMACD	VMACD
Sherry	VMACD	VMACD	VMACD	VMACD	VMACD
Laura	VMACD	VMACD	VMACD	VMACD	VMACD

Acronym: VMACD
Vocabulary – use scientific vocabulary appropriately
Material – use scientific materials safely
Assistance – asks for assistance when appropriate
Collaborates – collaborates with group member to engage in scientific investigation
Data – collects data using appropriate units, measures, and structures

Example 5: *Grade 7 mathematics teachers worked together to develop a description of success. This served as the explanation about what "proficiency" on the report card actually entailed. (See Figure 3-10.) The teachers collected a range of evidence based on classroom work; this evidence varied from student to student. They also included the results of school-wide assessments. As the individual teacher then examined all of the evidence, he made a professional judgment about whether proficiency was being met and the degree to which each math student was meeting expectations, approaching expectations, and requiring on-going help.*

In the following accounts, teachers use narrative comments as their reporting format.

Figure 3-10 ▼

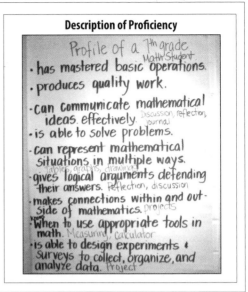

Description of Proficiency

Example 1: *In a Kindergarten through Grade 8 school, teachers created a visual continuum in the area of writing. Over the course of a year and after a school-wide writing task, these teachers placed student writing samples into a progression that illustrated the "very next step" in the writing process. In essence, they filled the "gaps" that commercial or provincial exemplars from grade-level writing rubrics miss. Each sample was accompanied with statements that described what was "present" in the writing. (See Figure 3-11.) The writing continuum was used to support instruction, cycles of feedback to the students, and self- and peer assessment. At the end of each term, teachers incorporated the statements into narrative comments for report cards. Teachers were thus able to use language with which the students were intimately familiar to describe strengths and areas for growth and progress.*

Example 2: *Mrs. H is required to do narrative report cards. In preparation for writing the comments, she listed all of the specific learning outcomes that she focused on during the term. She rewrote them in parent-friendly language. For each student, Mrs. H listed the outcomes that he or she has accomplished and those that need further attention or development. She deliberately illustrated several of the outcomes with simple examples. (See Figure 3-12.)*

Figure 3-11 ▼

Beginning of a K-6 Writing Continuum

With thanks to Westbrook School, Alberta.

Narrative Report Card Comments

Strengths/Accomplishments:

- She reads chapter books with fluency and improving expression (Red Alert).
- She uses a selection of strategies to read unknown words including skip reading, blending, framing, picture clues, and predicting.
- She reads for a purpose, researches a topic, and applies these skills to write key words to describe the appearance of a dinosaur.
- She can give the main elements of a complex story plot including title, illustrator, author, characters, main events, problem, and solution.
- She is developing skills in interpreting a character profile through the creation of character voices.
- She writes longer sequentially developed stories involving a beginning with setting and character introductions, more relevant supportive details and descriptive language, conversations, a description of events leading to a main climactic problem, and a simple ending.
- She is able to complete the grammar and word study activities with increasing ease.
- She can compare and contrast story elements of more than one title by the same author.
- Her personal spelling demonstrates a working knowledge of consonants, blends, short vowels, some long vowels with silent 'e', some vowel partners, and some familiar words.
- She can add and subtract numbers to 20 with reasonable speed and accuracy.
- She can give the place value of numbers to 999 in terms of hundreds, tens, and ones and expanded notation (4 hundreds, 7 tens and 9 ones $= 400 + 70 + 9 = 479$).
- She is learning to add with regrouping using an algorithm ($278 + 106$).
- She can independently skip count using more complex number patterns (by hundreds: 341, 441, 541).
- She can independently solve mathematical problems using critical, logical, and creative thinking skills.
- She can add and subtract three digit numbers without regrouping.
- She is developing dancing, skating, and fitness skills to enhance endurance and balance.

Areas Requiring Further Attention or Development:

I have no concerns regarding _____'s academic and personal development at this time.

Goals for Support for Learning:

Goals:
- To write in different genres
- To read over her written drafts to edit familiar spelling patterns, especially word endings (stopping, stopped), capitalization, and punctuation.

Support for learning:
Teacher will underline errors in capitalization, punctuation, and common spelling/patterns to edit.

_____ is encouraged to:
- Read from different genres to develop a repertoire of plot structures
- Re-read her written drafts and check for spelling, capitalization, and punctuation errors.

Her parents can help her to edit her personal writings at home.

Summary:

_____ is making excellent progress in all areas of her academic and personal development. She easily meets the widely-held expectations for her age at this time and reads and writes beyond grade-level. She is to be commended on her significant achievements and outstanding efforts.

With thanks to Sylvia Hurford, British Columbia.

Example 3: *Mrs. H communicates through narrative comments both the goals that are set out for each student for the coming term and the goals that the student had been focusing on during the current term. This deliberate inclusion of last term's goals serves to remind everyone about where the student was before moving on to the next steps in the learning. Goals include the ones that the students set for themselves, as well as the ones set by Mrs. H. (See Figure 3-13.)*

Figure 3-13 ▼

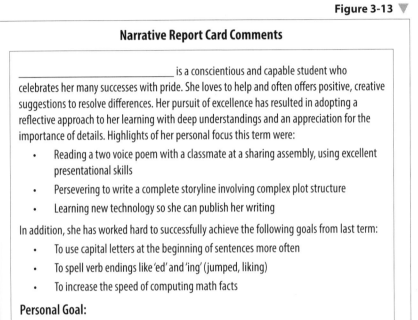

Narrative Report Card Comments

_____ is a conscientious and capable student who celebrates her many successes with pride. She loves to help and often offers positive, creative suggestions to resolve differences. Her pursuit of excellence has resulted in adopting a reflective approach to her learning with deep understandings and an appreciation for the importance of details. Highlights of her personal focus this term were:

- Reading a two voice poem with a classmate at a sharing assembly, using excellent presentational skills
- Persevering to write a complete storyline involving complex plot structure
- Learning new technology so she can publish her writing

In addition, she has worked hard to successfully achieve the following goals from last term:

- To use capital letters at the beginning of sentences more often
- To spell verb endings like 'ed' and 'ing' (jumped, liking)
- To increase the speed of computing math facts

Personal Goal:

- To learn how to do harder subtraction wheels

With thanks to Sylvia Hurford, British Columbia.

When we evaluate, we determine the worth, or value, of the evidence; we appraise it with respect to excellence, or merit. Simply totalling the marks or grades in our record books means that important evidence may not be considered, and learning and achievement will therefore not be accurately represented in the evaluation. When evaluating, teachers must be especially careful as they work with numbers from performance scales and rubrics. Totalling scores from rubrics and averaging them with other kinds of numbers is like adding mangoes, potatoes, apples, and trees. It does not make mathematical sense. After all, a great score on a quiz that focuses on simple mathematical operations is not equal to work that involves the kind of complex problem-solving that contains multiple operations and explanations of the choices made along the way.

After the report card has been prepared, it is time to involve students in communicating with others about their learning.

4. Involving Students in the Reporting Process

Formal evaluating and reporting is usually required by legislation or policy and is a process of looking at the evidence, having conversations and conferences about what the evidence means, and keeping a written record of the evaluation for each learner's permanent file. Reporting used to be an event that happened only at set times in a year. Now, in many jurisdictions, examining and making sense of a student's learning is becoming an ongoing process that involves students, parents, and teachers.

It is not only teachers who have the responsibility for evaluating and reporting. Students and parents, too, have a role. Students do the learning and create evidence along the way. In preparation for evaluation and reporting, students organize their evidence of learning and summarize their strengths, needs, and plans for more learning. They present the evidence to account for their learning to others and receive feedback. Then they set goals for future learning. Parents, legal guardians, or other adults selected by the student, participate by looking at the evidence, by listening, watching, asking questions, and making sense of the evidence in relation to the standards. They interpret the evidence and the accompanying self-assessments that students present; they consider the commentary given by the teacher. When students and their parents are engaged in reviewing the evidence and affirming whether or not the evaluation makes sense, sound professional judgments by teachers are more likely to be made, simply because information has been provided by others.

Every time students speak with their parents about learning, they are reporting. For example, whenever students take home a sample of their work and discuss it or invite parents to a portfolio afternoon to look at their work, they are reporting to parents about their learning. Increasingly, teachers are involving even the youngest students in the conferencing and reporting process and inviting them and their parents to be part of student-parent-teacher conferences. The purpose of these conferences is to look at the evidence, highlight strengths, consider and discuss areas needing improvement, and set goals.

In the following accounts, students are deeply involved in communicating their learning to others:

Example 1: *In the third term, as there is no in-school parent-teacher-student conference, Ms. N's students, (see p. 48 for earlier description of "proof cards"), take folders that are filled with their work and the proof cards home to share with their parents. Because each sample of work has been selected by the students to provide specific evidence of quality and proficiency in mathematics for this term, they are already prepared to communicate; they have been the ones to select and reflect on what they have learned in relation to the expectations.*

Example 2: *An early and middle years school hosts parent-teacher-student conferences before the report cards are written and published. Though the structure in each class varies from teacher to teacher, core tenets exist. Students demonstrate their learning to parents in "real time." This may include reading a passage from a text at their instructional level, solving a math problem with which they can have success, sharing a piece of writing from a content area, and going through an inquiry report from their social studies class. During their conversation with the teacher, the parents are shown work that would best represent the approximation of what work at this time of year could look like, given a trajectory to end-of-year outcomes. Parents are now able to use this experience as context when they read the report card that is sent home two weeks after these conferences.*

Example 3: *A Kindergarten teacher, Mrs. R, expects parents to bring their children to the parent-teacher conference. Students spend about 40 minutes taking their parents around the room to describe or demonstrate what they do each day. Mrs. R provides a guide for the students that uses picture and word cues about what is to come next. (Families begin about ten minutes after each other, so there are two to four families in the room at one time.) Students:*

- *read a book at their instructional level to their parents.*
- *share a piece of math work that has been identified in their math folder with a bright sticky note.*
- *read a piece of writing from their journal that has been identified with a bright sticky note.*
- *use math manipulatives to count out the number of days that they have been in school.*
- *talk through the calendar, which includes the month, days of the week, and the concepts of yesterday, today, and tomorrow.*
- *show their parents software that they are using at the computer station.*
- *take them outside to the Kindergarten garden.*

The parents and students then meet with the teacher to engage in additional conversation and reflection. As the parents and students finish, they sit down at a table and complete a reflection frame that includes the following prompts (See Figure 3-14.):

- *What you liked about the time in the classroom today…*
- *What is one thing that surprised you about your child?*
- *In what ways do you feel informed about your child's progress?*
- *What suggestions might you have for our next parent-student-teacher conferences?*

▼ Figure 3-14

Parent and child reflecting on conference

With thanks to Riley and her mother, Hawai'i.

Example 4: *In the areas of physical education, practical and applied arts, and the visual, performing, and musical arts, students can prepare a performance or a demonstration to be done at home. This performance or demonstration would highlight something that the student can do now as a result of the learning during the term. (See Figure 3-15.)*

▼ Figure 3-15

Home Performances

Students perform a skill at home for family members.
The audience listens and comments on the performance.

1. Ask students to arrange to perform a specific task or skill they have learned in class (for example, a cooking or art technique, poetry presentation, movement exercise, computer or sports skill) for someone at home.

2. Give students a form to complete that highlights three things the performer would like the audience to observe.

3. At the time of the performance, have students give their audience the form, explaining what they would like them to observe. Students perform their task or skill.

4. After the performance, students ask their audience for a response.

Home Performance by _____Reg_____

I am going to _play four Strong Winds on the guitar_

Please notice:
- that this piece is easy to play
- I know 4 chords — C G7 Dm7 F
- I can change chords quickly.

Date_April 11_

Audience Response by _____Alanna_____

After listening to and watching your performance I'd like to compliment you on: _excellent playing of the piece and playing it all the way through._

I'd also like to add: _You are getting better._

_____

© Gregory, Cameron & Davies (2011) *Conferencing and Reporting*, 2nd Edition, p. 33.

As we stated earlier, teachers' professional lives might be simpler if evaluating and reporting could be tidy and "objective." However, the process of making evaluations informed by a teacher's professional judgment is inherently subjective. The more reliable and valid the evidence collected and the longer the period of time over which it is collected, the more confident everyone can be in their professional judgment. By looking for patterns and trends over time, based on multiple sources (triangulation) of reliable and valid evidence, teachers can report with confidence.

As we focus on summative, end-of-term grading and reporting, it is important that we revisit the evidence that was collected during the learning – evidence that was formative in nature. It is critical that classroom teachers review all the evidence of learning collected over time in order to make an informed professional judgment. The Assessment Reform Group put it this way, "Innumerable classroom events enable teachers to gather information about pupils by observing, questioning, listening to informal discussions and reviewing written work. In formative assessment this information may be used immediately to help pupils or it may be stored and used to plan future learning opportunities. . . For formative assessment, the evidence is interpreted in relation to the progress of a pupil towards the goals of a particular section of work. Next steps are decided according to what has been achieved and what problems have been encountered. The interpretation is in terms of *what to do to help further learning*, not what level or grade a pupil has reached" (ARG, 2006, pp. 9, 10).

Teachers assist students in collecting and showing proof of their learning. They support students as they communicate their learning with parents. Teachers make themselves available to discuss how they have evaluated the student's work and to discuss with parents the ways that their child's learning could be better supported. In the end, teachers are the final arbitrators and evaluators of their students' work. This is our professional responsibility.

Now that you have exercised your professional judgment and have reported on your students' learning and achievement, it is important to reflect on the entire process and take time to research, refine, revise . . . and start again.

Afterword: Until the Next Time

"Get over the idea that only children should spend their time in study. Be a student so long as you still have something to learn, and this will mean all your life."

Henry L. Doherty

We began by stating that we would demonstrate the "simplicity that lies beyond complexity." To that end, we started with two accounts – one from Kindergarten and another from Grade 7. Both included what some might say was a deceptively simple learning strategy – placing a blue sticky note on a part of the work that proved the student could now do something that he or she was earlier unable to do and using different colours to prove alignment with co-constructed criteria. While simple, these ideas have at their core a belief that students are partners in the learning process, not passive by-standers who, if they are lucky, can guess at what we expect and do it right the first time.

This belief has led us to work alongside teachers and leaders across North America and beyond to bring clarity to the complex task of classroom assessment, evaluation, and reporting. And along that journey, we have learned from them – more than these pages can hold. That said, we know that classroom assessment is complicated by the context in which it takes place: the students with whom we work, our colleagues, time constraints, regulations and policies, outside mandates, and more. As professionals, we are always doing the best we can given what we know, so it is important that we continue to learn and be informed. We then are able to continuously revise and refine what we do.

Between now and the next time you engage in classroom assessment and reporting, consider:

- reflecting on what is working, what is not, and possible next steps towards continued improvement.

- researching more about classroom assessment, evaluation, and reporting.

- conducting an inquiry into your classroom assessment, evaluation, and reporting practices.

- writing your own narrative to deepen your understanding and better prepare you to support the growing understanding of others.
- working with colleagues to build shared understanding of quality and success in relation to standards or learning outcomes.

As you learn more and inform your professional judgment through reflection, research, and ongoing collegial conversations, your students will benefit. And, in the end, that is what matters. After all, none of us are in education for the "big bucks;" we are in education to make a difference. And, research from around the world (Norway, 2011; Fredericton 2014) clearly documents the idea that classroom assessment has the greatest effect on learning and achievement of any education innovation ever documented.

It is as simple, and as complex, as that.

"Simplicity is the ultimate sophistication."
Clare Boothe Luce

References

Absolum, M. 2014. https://a4larchive.wordpress.com/delegates/absolum-michael/.

Assessment Reform Group (ARG). 2002. *Assessment for learning: 10 principles*. Pamphlet on research-based principles to guide classroom practice.

Assessment Reform Group (ARG). 2006. *The role of teachers in the assessment of learning*. Pamphlet produced by Assessment Systems for the Future project (ASF). http://arrts.gtcni.org.uk/gtcni/handle/2428/4617.

Black, P. and Wiliam, D. 1998. Inside the black box: Raising standards through classroom assessment. *Phi Delta Kappan* 80(2): pp. 1-20.

Burger, J., Perry, B., and Eagle, M. 2009. "Aggregating and analyzing classroom achievement data supplemental to external tests." In T.J. Kowalski and T.J. Lasley II (Eds.) *Handbook of Data-Based Decision Making in Education*. Routledge.

Butler, R. 1988. Enhancing and undermining intrinsic motivation: The effects of task-involving and ego-involving evaluation on interest. *British Journal of Educational Psychology* 58: pp. 1-14.

Covington, M.V. 1998. *The Will to Learn: A Guide for Motivating Young People*. Cambridge, UK: Cambridge University Press.

Crooks, T. 1988. The impact of classroom evaluation on students. *Review of Educational Research*, Vol. 58(4): pp. 438-481.

Cuthbert, P. 2014. New pedagogies for deeper learning. *MASS Journal*, Vol. 15(1): pp. 12-15.

Davies, A. 2004. *Facilitator's Guide to Classroom Assessment K-12* (Multimedia Resource). Courtenay, BC: Connections Publishing.

Davies. A. 2010. *Assessment for Learning K-12* – 2nd Edition of Workshop-in-a-Box (Multimedia Resource). Courtenay, BC: Connections Publishing

Davies, A. 2011. *Making Classroom Assessment Work,* 3rd Edition. Courtenay, BC: Connections Publishing and Bloomington, IN: Solution Tree Press.

Davies, A., Herbst, S., and Parrott Reynolds, B. 2012. *Transforming Schools and Systems Using Assessment: A Practical Guide.* Courtenay, BC: Connections Publishing and Bloomington, IN: Solution Tree Press.

Dufour, R., Dufour, R., Eaker, R., and Many, T. 2006. *Learning By Doing: A Handbook for Professional Learning Communities at Work.* Bloomington, IN: Solution Tree.

Glaude, C. 2005. *Protocols for Professional Learning Conversations.* Courtenay, BC: Connections Publishing and Bloomington, IN: Solution Tree Press.

Glaude, C. 2010. *When Students Fail to Learn: Protocols for a School-Wide Response.* Courtenay, BC: Connections Publishing and Bloomington, IN: Solution Tree Press.

Gordon, S. and Reese, M. 1997. High stakes testing: Worth the price? *Journal of School Leadership* 7: pp. 345-368.

Gregory, K., Cameron, C., and Davies, A. 2011. *Conferencing and Reporting,* 2nd Edition. Courtenay, BC: Connections Publishing and Bloomington, IN: Solution Tree Press.

Gregory, K., Cameron, C., and Davies, A. 2011. *Self-Assessment and Goal Setting,* 2nd Edition. Courtenay, BC: Connections Publishing and Bloomington, IN: Solution Tree Press.

Gregory, K., Cameron, C., and Davies, A. 2011. *Setting and Using Criteria,* 2nd Edition. Courtenay, BC: Connections Publishing and Bloomington, IN: Solution Tree Press.

Harlen, W. and Deakin Crick, R. 2002a. A systematic review of the impact of summative assessment and tests on students' motivation for learning (EPPI-Centre Review, version 1.1*) In: *Research Evidence in Education Library.* London; EPPI-Centre, Social Science Research Unit, Institute of Education.

Harlen, W. and Deakin Crick, R. 2002b. *Testing, Motivation, and Learning.* Pamphlet produced by Assessment Reform Group at University of Cambridge Faculty of Education.

Herbst, S. and Davies, A. 2014. *A Fresh Look at Grading and Reporting in High Schools.* Courtenay, BC: Connections Publishing and Bloomington, IN: Solution Tree Press.

Lincoln, Y. and Guba, E. 1984. *Naturalistic Inquiry.* Beverly Hills, CA: SAGE.

Looney, J. 2005. *Formative Assessment – Improving Learning in Secondary Classrooms.* London, UK: OECD Publishing.

McCluskey, L. 2003. Video Presentation. In Alberta Assessment Consortium's ReFocus – The St. Paul School Story.

Ministry of Education-Ontario. 2010. *Growing Success: Assessment, Evaluation, and Reporting in Ontario Schools.* http://www.edu.gov.on.ca.

Reay, D. and Wiliam, D. 1999. 'I'll be a nothing': Structure, agency and the construction of identity through assessment. *British Educational Research Journal* 25(3): pp. 343-354.

Roderick M. and Engel, M. 2001. The grasshopper and the ant: Motivational response of low achieving pupils to high stakes testing. *Educational Evaluation and Policy Analysis* 23(3): pp. 197-228.

Stiggins, R. 2002. Assessment crisis: The absence of assessment for learning. *Phi Delta Kappan* 83(10): pp. 758-765, June 2002.

Stiggins, R. 2013. *Foreword; Quality Assessment in High School: Accounts from Teachers,* edited by A. Davies, S. Herbst, and K. Busick. Courtenay, BC; Connections Publishing and Bloomington, IN: Solution Tree Press.

Stiggins, R. and Bridgeford, N. 1985. The ecology of classroom assessment. *Journal of Educational Measurement,* Vol. 22(4): pp. 271–286, December 1985.

Appendix A: From Reporting to Informing: Students and the Language of Assessment[1]

Reporting is a hot topic in educational circles today. It is important for parents to be informed about their child's learning and achievement in school. Many jurisdictions are revisiting their evaluation, grading, and reporting practices. In the past, the options were limited to report cards using a symbol system – codes such as A, B, 84%, 3 – that were sent home periodically. Parents and teachers met to interpret the information and provide additional information face-to-face.

Things are changing. Today a printed report card and an online grading program have ceased to be the only, or even the best, options for informing parents about student learning. Districts may still use online grading programs and other similar technology as part of their student management system, but many are questioning their value in reporting to parents. It just doesn't make sense to limit the information flow to numerical data.

These days inexpensive, well-designed technology is making the flow of continuous, high-quality information possible – e-Pearl from Concordia University, SeeSaw, Evernote, and Fresh Grade are just a few examples. Students upload evidence of their learning such as work samples, audio and video recordings, self-assessments, and so on in real time. Peers, teachers, parents, and others can view the evidence of learning and give just-in-time feedback. In teachers' hands, these tools change the conversation because the evidence of learning no longer needs to be "encoded" and available only three or four times a year. And, when students are deeply involved in the classroom assessment process, they have the language of assessment and are able to explain what they have learned and how they know they have learned it.

---

1   Adapted from Anne Davies and Sandra Herbst blogspot, May 7, 2014 posting http://annedavies.blogspot.ca/2014/05/from-reporting-to-informing-students.html

When one considers how curriculum has expanded in breadth and depth, it makes sense that reporting is moving beyond marks, numbers, and grades. Learning outcomes are complex. For example, most policy documents talk about evidence of student learning being triangulated – from multiple sources over time. Since evidence of learning is potentially anything a child does, says, or creates, it makes sense that students and teachers would find ways to use this evidence to demonstrate learning and achievement in an ongoing way – in a way that continuously informs parents.

On April 12, 2014, during the *Assessment for Learning: Canada in Conversation with the World* Conference at the University of New Brunswick in Fredericton, NB, Michael Absolum from New Zealand shared the following information (see Figure A-1) and talked about moving from reporting to informing. He spoke about one of the projects in New Zealand where they have been working to support schools to accelerate learning through using assessment in the service of learning. He also shared a video clip that included a Year 7 student, Jaime, talking about how he can help his parents know where he is in his learning and how they can help him learn. The school uses tablets and software that allow students to post, at any time during the learning, evidence of what they are able to do. At the same time, progressions or continua are also posted so that parents can see where their child's work is in relation to what the expectations are. (See Figure A-2 for a transcript of Jaime's portion of the video.) Please notice the point where the student talks about his

▼ **Figure A-1**

School Initiative – Changing the Purposes	
From *Reporting*	**To *Informing***
Reporting to you, as parent, what your child has learnt/achieved	Sharing information and the understanding of that information
Focussed on success/failure learning of student	Focussed on supporting progress and achievement
Learning is not the purpose	Better learning by **all** is the purpose
Essentially a one-way message Take it or leave it	Collaborating and co-constructing the way forward
Once or twice a year	Continuous and timely
From school to parent	Multi-layered and multi-directional with student, parents, whānau, teacher, school all in conversation
Technology improves the quality and richness of the information and of the Information flows	

© 2014 Michael Absolum www.evaluate.co.nz

responsibility to inform parents using evidence, "...anything to kind of prove, yes I can do this. This is an example of how I've done it." Michael Absolum summarized by noting that teachers saw a significant shift occurring when students were able to articulate the important ideas – when they could inform others about their learning on an ongoing basis, not just at three or four prescribed times during the year.

▼ **Figure A-2**

Partial Transcript of Video "Our Parents Know Where We Are At and Can Help Us Learn"

Sarah Martin, Principal
Parents have a view into [their child's] learning and can, in partnership, see exactly where the child is and what their next steps are. They also get a good look at what the child has achieved and where that lines up to being at a standard or not.

Jaime, Student
We used to have the progressions just on paper and so when you are in green you need to learn something and then you move to yellow. But we have recently put it onto our sites on the Internet and so using that, our parents can ask us whenever they want to see what we have been learning and, you know, what we have done and to kind of prove that we have learned it...on several pieces of it we add evidence and that could be anything from just a photo to a video to a recording to a slideshow – just anything to kind of prove, "Yes I can do this and this is an example of how I have done it."

Sarah Martin, Principal
So a parent can very clearly see where an expectation is after 40 weeks of school or after two or three or four years at school and whether or not their child is at that standard or above or below that standard.

Jaime, Student
Because everything that we do here is interesting, instead of just going home as you would from a typical school and your parents would ask, "What did you do today?"..."Ah, nothing." You come home and you can say "I made some good progress in literacy. I got a good result. Or I had good fun in [shops] today. We managed to get all our souvenirs made. You tell them what you have done and because they can also see it [it is different than] only knowing about what you have learned at the end of the year when they get a report saying, "This is where your child is at..." They can go online and see the progression... this is end of the year 7 and they are working up there and they know this and they can tell where you are.

Used with permission
Taken from http://www.evaluate.co.nz/parents-help-learn/

At the heart of these present and emerging technologies are students who know the language of assessment and students who can provide evidence of their own learning. This is a "game-changer" because suddenly students have the language to articulate what they have learned, what they need to learn, and what their next steps are. They can be actual partners in the informing process. Students are more specific and are able to show their learning more thoroughly and thoughtfully than with a report card, distributed three times a year.

An example of this comes from Lisa McCluskey (2003), an early childhood educator working in Edmonton, who deliberately supported students to "learn the language of assessment." In one video clip, Sarah, a five-year-old student, describes what writers at different points in their writing development do. As she points to one of the writing samples, Sarah says, "This is where I am. I sound it out. I try to keep them nicely written. I try to make the right words. I try to keep the letters with a space before they start. And I'm going over here (pointing to the next writing sample in the continuum)." This is a powerful example of students learning the language of assessment. This is what enables students to become partners in the assessment process.

In a Grade 8 science class, Lisa Hogan expects her students to use the language of quality to self-assess their work. While being videotaped, a male student says, "We're supposed to tell her what quality work it is – whether we think it is high- quality work or low-quality work. She needs to see why we think that. So those arrows, we move them to where we think the quality work is and type in the arrow what the quality work is. Here I have complete sentences. Over here I use correct punctuation and spelling. Just so she knows we know what we've done is quality work."

As we reflect on all of these examples, we are again struck by the importance of students learning the language of assessment. Whether you consider self-regulation, co-regulation, metacognition, student-involved moderation of work samples, self-assessment, peer assessment, embedded formative assessment, motivation, engagement, instructional rubrics, or some other aspect of deep student involvement in the assessment process, it is clear. Language is the great connector. Students need to learn the language of assessment. And this means they need to be taught. Without it, leveraging other applications like Explain Everything, Show Me, or Educreations will fall flat. Technology is viewed as an accelerator of learning (Cuthbert, 2014) and, from that viewpoint, can prove both helpful and essential in the continuous informing of parents. Yet we need to ensure that students can be able partners in that endeavour.

Instead of simplifying the evidence of learning to mere quantitative measures, the evidence is expanded to show more of the learning. The qualitative evidence – the messy stuff – can be included because students are also involved. And that evidence of learning can be used to show "proof" of what students know, where they are in their learning, what they're learning next, and what help is needed to make a difference (Herbst & Davies, 2014). And technology, instead of limiting the information to numerical data, "improves the quality and richness of the information and helps the information flow" (Absolum, 2014). Reporting becomes transformed as students work with teachers to "inform" their parents, themselves, and others.

Appendix B: Digging Deeper— What About These Challenges?[1]

In our work with schools, systems, and organizations, we have often been confronted with "yah buts" or "push backs" to the ideas and research of assessment and evaluation. Over the years, patterns and trends have emerged and so we have provided responses to some of the most common ones. Some might view these "yah buts" or "push backs" as negative or argumentative. Rather, we view them as opportunities to engage in dialogue – to seek to understand the viewpoints of others before we ourselves reach full understanding.

We are deliberately including them in this elementary resource for the following reasons:

- Some colleagues at the elementary level may, in fact, express similar concerns.

- Colleagues from the secondary level may share these concerns with colleagues at the elementary level. Parents and community members may also voice these very points during parent council meetings, parent-student-teacher-conferences, or other interactions. It is helpful have possible pathways of response, rather than simply acquiescing to the stated point of view.

- Alignment of understanding across a K-12 system is vitally important. Recognizing and coming to realize issues at other levels strengthens systemic conversation and action.

Please note that these responses are not meant to be comprehensive in nature. They serve as a starting point for continued and informed discussion and dialogue.

---

1   Appendix B is reprinted, with slight adaptions, from the book *A Fresh Look at Grading and Reporting in High Schools* (Herbst & Davies, 2014).

Push Back 1: Assessment isn't about helping my students learn. It is something that comes at the end of learning.

Some teachers used to think that assessment is a test, performance task, or culminating assignment that has to be done at the end of a unit so that the class can move to the next topic and a grade can be entered into a grade book. It is considered an event or a thing. Classroom assessment is understood better now. Now we know that assessment *for* learning occurs during the learning. We let students know what the learning target or destination is, we share with them what success and quality look like, and we provide them (or they provide themselves) with specific and descriptive feedback so that they can adjust what they are doing to get to that learning target. These strategies definitely help students learn. Also, many teachers use effective classroom assessment strategies to support student learning, but think they are simply powerful instructional techniques.

Assessment *of* learning – evaluation or summative assessment – occurs at the end of the learning. It is the time when we make a professional judgment. It comes at the end of the learning, when time has run out. It occurs when teachers make a decision and communicate to others the degree to which or the level at which content and the processes that compose the course have been learned.

The research of the Assessment Reform Group (2002, 2006) is clear in its findings. Involving students in their assessment makes a significant difference in the achievement levels of students.

How else might you respond to this "Push Back"?

Push Back 2: This process of determining how well students are doing may make sense at the elementary level, but at the secondary level we are preparing our students for university or college. This does not work in the real world.

It is true. Some of our students do continue their education immediately after high school graduation by attending college or university. But not all our students follow this pathway, and among those who do start, many do not continue into the second, third, and fourth years. So, while it is important to help students to see themselves continuing on to postsecondary institutions, if that is their dream, high school is a time for students to practice and put patterns of behaviour in place that will be helpful later on, whether at university, college, the workplace, or in the community. Learning the skill of self-monitoring and self-regulating their way to success is extremely important. It is necessary that students understand what needs to be done, how their current work aligns with what needs to be done, and how they can close the gap between the two, especially outside the K-12 setting.

How else might you respond to this "Push Back"?

Push Back 3: At the high school level, there are high-stakes tests. This is true at the elementary level, in some jurisdictions. So I can't afford to involve my students in this way.

This is a good point. Many teachers feel the pressure of external and internal exams. It is an ever-present reality, not only in the high school. However, involving students in their own assessment – helping them to understand what is expected of them, helping them picture quality by sharing samples or co-constructing criteria, and helping them to self-monitor to success – actually prepares them for those exams and tests. Research shows that students who are involved in assessment *for* learning strategies do better on external tests and measures than those who are not (Rodriguez, 2004; Meisels et al., 2003).

Furthermore, the research indicates that students whose teachers spend all their time "teaching to the test" score lower on those same external tests and measures (e.g., Berliner& Biddle, 1998; Darling-Hammond & Richardson, 2009). Assessment for student learning prepares students for whatever comes their way by helping them deeply understand the work that is expected of them.

And finally, high-stakes tests most often comprise only a portion of the entire course grade – rarely 100% of it. Therefore the class grade can be the part of the overall grade that evaluates the standards and outcomes that the high-stakes test did not and evaluates them in ways that the high-stakes test cannot. For example, involving students in collecting triangulated evidence of learning, engaging them in feedback loops, and having them talk about their learning are just a few of the ways that we can ensure that the class portion of the final grade is as reliable and valid as possible.

How else might you respond to this "Push Back"?

Push Back 4: Secondary curricula are jammed with standards and expectations. I don't have time to do all of this with my students.

We recently heard a high school mathematics teacher say this aloud in a group of dozens of high school colleagues. A colleague turned to him and commented that he couldn't believe that the high school curriculum was more packed than that at the elementary level. He continued by stating that many kindergarten teachers deal with students who come to school not knowing even how to hold pencils or scissors; if students are lacking such basic skills as these, then there truly is a lot to cover.

Teachers have noted that when they involve students in their own assessment, they save time. For example, at the beginning of a semester, a high school physics teacher co-constructed criteria with his students about what counted in a lab report, based on sample reports from previous years. He recognized that the lab reports that he received from his students after that process were what he would usually see closer to the end of the semester. He reasoned that he had just saved months of teaching time. Now he could teach concepts and curriculum standards earlier in the semester because he had "found time" that had, in the past, been spent going over and over what he expected from his students. At the elementary level, the same is true. Inquiry into questions about a writing form or math problem solving sets the stage for everyone's learning.

How else might you respond to this "Push Back"?

Push Back 5: Tests and quizzes are the only way to make sure that our assessment is objective and fair. All this other stuff is too subjective.

Tests and exams are only one way to see what a student knows. We do not say that tests, quizzes, and exams are not useful. However, not everything that is expected of students in the curriculum can be measured by a test. For example, students cannot be evaluated by a paper-and-pencil test in curriculum areas where they are expected to communicate orally. Additionally, a student may be able to demonstrate deep understanding in alternate and differentiated ways – just not solely on tests and the like.

Let us be clear. Tests are not objective measures. They usually result in scores that represent a quantitative measuring system related to numbers, which is as close as a test comes to being objective. Think about this: Two teachers might be preparing a test for the same unit of study. One teacher creates a test of 12 questions that appeal to her and the other teacher builds a test of five different questions that have served him well in the past. By selecting questions that they view to be important, these two teachers have built in subjectivity.

Instead of asking ourselves whether our measures are objective, we need to be asking ourselves whether our measures are reliable and valid. Reliability refers to repeatability. Can the student show what he knows in different situations and at different times?

Validity refers to the match of the evidence of learning to what is to be assessed – what is to be learned. And, to illustrate further, let us go back to the example of an oral presentation. We cannot evaluate whether a student can orally communicate ideas to an audience by asking them to complete a paper-and-pencil test. From a classroom assessment perspective, this evidence of learning is not valid, given what was to be learned.

Teacher professional judgment is more reliable and valid than external tests when teachers have been involved in examining student work, co-constructing criteria, scoring the work, and checking for inter-rater reliability (ARG, 2006, Burger et al., 2009). Inter-rater reliability is defined as the result of learning to make an informed professional judgment. Educators engage in a process of inter-rater reliability when they meet, create quality criteria, and build a scoring rubric for student work. The student work could include, for example, a performance task, a product, observations of application, or a body of evidence. Each educator examines and then scores the student work using a scoring rubric. At this point, all the scores are examined for consistency among all the educators. The percentage to which they agree is used to determine inter-rater reliability. The higher the percentage of agreement among all the educators' rating (i.e., the more the scores are similar), the higher the inter-rater reliability will be. This process helps teachers refine and improve their professional judgment.

How else might you respond to this "Push Back"?

Push Back 6: We need to make sure that our assessment and evaluations are fair, and that means that we need to use all the same assignments, tests, and tasks to determine a grade or mark for all of our students.

State and provincial standards, outcomes, or curriculum expectations identify targets that students need to reach, but they do not specify how students are to reach them. For example, according to the curriculum, outcome, or standard, a student must be able to describe a certain scientific concept. It does not, however, state that the concept needs to be described only by the written word. Some students might be able to describe it in conversation or by using a labelled diagram. In other words, there is more than one way for students to show what they know.

To use a highly quoted phrase – fair is not always equal. Educators come to the profession and to the signing of their first contract in many different ways. Some teachers come to the profession after having worked for many years in another field. Yet others come to teaching through the more direct route of university or college right after high school. And still others come back to teaching after time spent raising a family, taking a sabbatical, or travelling around the world. Few of us would say that the only teacher who deserves a contract is the one who has taken the direct route. However, this same understanding is not always extended to our students. Some would say that the way to a grade on a transcript or a report card is to be travelled in exactly the same way in order for it to be fair.

We need to focus on providing all students with the opportunity to learn and to show what they have learned in a way that best connects to their own learning needs and strengths; we need to make this appropriate and sufficient, given what students need to know, do, and articulate as outlined in the curriculum standards or outcomes. We need to check if the student understands and can articulate that understanding. It is in the articulation that differing forms can be taken. It is not fair to say that a student does not understand the effect of modern war on society, for example, simply because he or she cannot write it down. It becomes equitable if that student has the opportunity to articulate that understanding in different ways, instead of only putting pen to paper.

How else might you respond to this "Push Back"?

Push Back 7: Being involved in their own assessment makes sense when teachers are working with students who "get it." It just does not work with students who struggle.

In this area, the research is exceedingly clear. Quality classroom assessment has the largest effect on student achievement ever documented (Black and Wiliam, 1998, 2003; Black, P. et al., 2003). This is true for all students, and it is especially true for students who struggle academically.

From a practical point of view, this makes absolute sense. Students who struggle often do so because they do not intuitively know, or cannot "read between the lines" to determine what the teacher wants. In every class, there are students who seem to be able to learn without very much direction or instruction. However, it seems as though this kind of student in our schools is diminishing. More and more, our students need explicit information that describes what is expected of them. Students who struggle do not get enough to "go on" from comments like "Try harder," "You can do better," or "I will give you time to re-do this work." They need specific information to better understand what the work needs to look like, what counts as quality, and what in their work is correct and what needs to be changed. Sharing samples with students and providing them with criteria about what counts in the work or assignment is crucial. This is assessment *for* learning.

How else might you respond to this "Push Back"?

Push Back 8: Only test scores and marks motivate students. We need to give them more of that. They need that kind of information.

Many of us believe that the best way to motivate others and ourselves is with external rewards like test scores, grades, and marks. This thinking can be a mistake. Research and writing in the area of human motivation (Pink, 2009; Covington, 1998) reports that what motivates us is the deeply human need to direct our own lives, to learn and create new things, and to do better by our world and ourselves. Edward Deci & Richard Ryan (2002) and Wynne Harlen & Ruth Deakin Crick (2002a, 2002b) remind us that extrinsic rewards alone – like test scores, grades, and marks, which are all forms of evaluative feedback – undermine interest and motivation.

Students who are fed a steady diet of evaluative feedback tend to select tasks that are low in difficulty, with an eye to getting them done as quickly and as easily as possible. For students who struggle, receiving evaluative feedback alone can lead to feelings of rejection and alienation. Consistent messaging that they are not doing well enough does not give them the information that they need to change what they are doing. Many students have difficulty decoding what the evaluative feedback is saying. What have I done well? What do I need to change?

How else might you respond to this "Push Back"?

Push Back 9: At the secondary level, I might see over 130 students in a semester. In the elementary school it is easier, because each teacher may only have 29 or 30 students. There is no time for me to do this.

What we know from the field of brain research is that even if we had a class with only one student, we would not be able to provide enough specific, descriptive feedback to maximize the learning. If we can't do it for one adequately, we can't do it for 131. So we need to involve the student. The student can give himself and his peers feedback. If we don't involve students, we miss valuable opportunities to provide feedback that can move the learning forward.

Some teachers do have over 130 students in their classes in one semester. Others have more than 500 in a week. This can be a challenge for some teachers, especially if each class they teach is from a different discipline or at a different level. Consider, though, the elementary teacher who might have 32 students in his class. He has to teach all 32 of those students English, mathematics, science, social studies, and health (and maybe more). Translated to a secondary school context, that would mean that that teacher could have 160 students over the semester. The demands from a curriculum perspective might not be all that different.

No matter what your context is, you can find benefits in improved student learning and can maximize the use of your time. After all, this is an ideal way to have students working harder than their teachers – and isn't the person working the hardest learning the most? Why shouldn't it be the students?

How else might you respond to this "Push Back"?

Push Back 10: It does not make sense to allow students the opportunity to re-do their work. They should only have one chance, and that is all.

Having the chance to do something again is viewed by some as shirking responsibility or reinforcing procrastination. But ask yourself this question: How many of your family, friends, and acquaintances required more than one attempt at getting their driver's license? Many people are not successful the first time, and yet the Motor Vehicle Branch allows them to come back and try again. What about if you failed a course at college or university? You were not kicked out of the entire program of study. You needed to try it again or attempt a different course. Why would we not extend the same opportunity to our secondary school-aged students?

When students remit their work a second or a third time, often after a round of specific and descriptive feedback, it is important that they indicate the way in which the work has changed. That is, as busy educators, we do not have time to review a piece of work a second time, to pore over that lab report, essay, or problem to realize only a surface, singular, or simple change has been made. Instead, students should be asked to prove to the teacher the ways in which that work is different and better aligned with the descriptions and expectations of quality. This might be accomplished by having the students either literally or virtually attach "sticky notes" to the spots where changes have been made. Or, this might mean that students indicate, in point form, what they did differently this time. Possibilities abound in order to allow this to happen. The key point is, though, that students have a shared responsibility with their teachers.

If we have given students feedback, can they consider it and produce the work, but at a higher level of achievement? Can we help students understand that we learn from our mistakes and the help that we have been given? Might we communicate to students that learning is lifelong and ongoing? These are important lessons.

How else might you respond to this "Push Back"?

Push Back 11: What about the students who don't do anything in class throughout the term or semester and then, at the end, hand most of their work in and show up to take the final exam? They pass based on work that is all done at the last moment. It's not right.

Some students have figured out that it is sometimes possible to pass in the last moments of the course. This can be frustrating. To change this, we need to re-examine our definition of success for the course. If we calculate a term or final mark based on only tests, quizzes, and a list of assignments, then, as we share this list with the students, they come to understand exactly what matters. It is only what is on the list. The learning outcomes and standards have effectively been replaced. Suddenly we have students who figure out how to give us exactly what we have asked for and no more. Some students may, in fact, only physically or figuratively "show up" around those events on that list.

What if teachers defined success in such a way that students had to collect evidence throughout the term to provide proof that they were reaching the learning goals set both for themselves and by the teacher? What if the evidence that they collect is evaluated and contributes to the end-of-term grade? What about a collection of evidence of learning – you might even choose to call it a portfolio – that at the end of the semester shows growth and development over time, in relation to important standards or outcomes? Could this comprehensive collection of evidence in relation to the standards and outcomes also be a significant part of the final grade?

What about describing what an A or a 90-percent-plus student would look like in this class? Could you include habits of mind such as perseverance, flexibility of thought, and risk-taking – the competencies often identified in the "front matter" of the curriculum? Could students show evidence of these habits of mind being evident day-by-day across the course and the semester? This is not only possible, but high school teachers have begun to share exactly how they do this (Davies, Herbst & Busick, 2013).

How else might you respond to this "Push Back"?

Push Back 12: What do I do with students who turn in their work late, or maybe not at all?

Teachers work with students to help them understand that they are responsible and have a role for providing evidence of their learning to the teacher. That is part of the students' role. Additionally, students need to understand that there are consequences for submitting their work late. However, the natural consequence of not handing in assignments should be to hand them in. Some people may think having to actually hand the work in is not a consequence or perhaps not enough of a consequence. We would agree, but it is the first step towards addressing the problem.

If the first reaction to work not being handed in is to begin to deduct marks, then very quickly students no longer see a reason to submit the missing evidence of learning. Currently, teachers are putting other things in place that serve as a consequence, including:

- setting up a student contract or referring students to additional supports

- chunking major assignments into smaller pieces that could be submitted in stages

- communicating with parents when assignments are due

- providing an alternate assignment that, while still meeting the intended outcomes of the original assignment, better reflects the student's interests and strengths

If evidence of learning is not available to the teacher, then a teacher's ability to make a professional judgment is impaired. If there is not enough evidence of learning, then a grade cannot be assigned. Teachers working with their colleagues have developed a variety of strategies to support students as they work to ensure students provide enough evidence of learning. At the end of the term, when report card grades are required, teachers need to be very careful that they are not putting themselves at professional risk. Report cards are legal documents. They report what students have learned and achieved in relation to the learning outcomes and standards for the course. If the records kept by the teacher show little or no evidence of learning in relation to the outcomes of the course, then the student grade must reflect what is not known. Some schools and systems use the abbreviation NE (which means Not Enough Evidence), and students have a certain length of time to submit the needed evidence or complete alternative tasks that give teachers enough evidence. If evidence is not available, then a grade is not assigned for the course – there is no credit recorded.

Sometimes it seems to be a matter of motivation. If our default stance is to deduct marks or assign a score of zero, then students might realize that there is no reason for them to turn in their work. This creates another set of problems that cannot be solved by penalties related to the grading system. The actual learning that has been accomplished is misrepresented by deductions. The baseline question is: Can/Does the student demonstrate mastery of the learning that is expected in the standards? Using zeros or reducing the grade because of behavioural factors is, as Rick Stiggins has pointed out, attacking classroom management and motivation challenges (Stiggins, 2005).

Some schools and systems continue to engage in lengthy and thoughtful discussions about these issues. Your discussions might be focused around the use of zeros, deducting marks for late assignments, or some other kind of response to students not providing the kind of evidence of learning requested. As you come to a collegial decision about these matters, we remind you that the final-grade calculation must reflect the informed professional judgment of the teacher and accurately represent a student's actual achievement.

As these issues are discussed, it is sometimes helpful to have an example from outside the situation to help us better understand the issues at hand. For example, some people say that in the real world, if things are late, there are consequences. What if a teacher does not complete the report cards by the specified date? Is she fired? No, she is not fired. Are her wages deducted? No, her wages are not deducted. What will happen? Likely, the principal will have a conversation with her to determine why the reports are not yet completed and to plan for next steps. This might mean bringing in a substitute so that the reports can be finished during the next school day, it might mean that a district consultant is brought in to provide support and guidance, or it might even mean that the principal spends the next two evenings sitting beside that teacher to ensure that they are done. The consequence for not doing report cards is doing report cards.

It is important for us to state very clearly that we do believe that there are instances that warrant the deduction of marks or the assignment of a zero. However, those two actions as default stances without some kind of intervention are difficult to support.

How else might you respond to this "Push Back"?

Push Back 13: Some parents don't value educators' professional judgment. Some even challenge what we record on a report card.

When parents question a teacher's informed professional judgment, teachers can choose to respond thoughtfully by engaging parents in conversation as they look at the relevant standards and samples. Samples have an important role to play in helping those outside the classroom understand the learning that is taking place. This is especially true for parents. Samples help us respond to the perennial parent question, "How is my child doing compared to the other students in the class?" The first thing we do is reframe the question so we can respond ethically. We say, "Your child, in relation to the standards or outcomes is . . . ," and we share samples of the current range of work and where their child's work is within that range. Samples also provide a strong visual to show parents how their child's work compares with what is expected.

Students also have a role to play. When they have been engaged as partners in this assessment process, collecting evidence and explaining why it is proof of learning, they are better able to explain to parents what the evidence means and what their next learning steps are.

How else might you respond to this "Push Back"?

Appendix C: Planning Questions

Preparing for Learning—Beginning with the End in Mind

1. Are all outcomes represented in the list?
2. In what ways does the list represent both process and product (do, say, know)?
3. Is each statement simple?

Collecting Evidence of Learning

1. In what ways will my evidence show whether or not students have learned what they needed to learn?
2. Is there any evidence that I am collecting for which I am not accountable?
3. Am I collecting evidence from multiple sources?
4. Am I collecting enough evidence to see patterns over time?
5. Am I collecting too much evidence? Is there something that I could stop collecting?
6. In what ways can my students be involved in collecting and organizing evidence of learning?

Describing Quality

1. Are samples available to show quality? Ways not to reach quality?
2. What are your plans to co-construct criteria?
3. Do you have a range of samples when learning is developmental?

Evaluation

1. Are report card grades given for the full range of educational standards or outcomes, not just those easiest to measure?
2. Has evidence of learning been selected because of its alignment with outcomes and standards?
3. Are the report card grades based upon a wide array of evidence from multiple sources over time so as to ensure validity and reliability?
4. Do students understand expectations and acceptable evidence?
5. Are students involved in co-constructing criteria in relation to products, processes, and collections of evidence of learning?
6. Does the summative evaluation take place after students have time and opportunity to learn?
7. Are report card grades derived from evidence present, not absent (thus devoid of practices such as assigning zeros, grading on a curve, averaging, or penalty deductions)?
8. Are report card grades for achievement of standards or learning outcomes reported separately from other nonachievement factors such as effort, attitude, attendance, and punctuality?
9. Are report card grades reflective of a student's most consistent, more recent pattern of performance in relation to course learning goals based on the relevant standards and outcomes, as well as pre-determined levels of quality?
10. Do report card grades reflect informed teacher professional judgment of the level of quality of student work in relation to the standards or outcomes?
11. Are report card grades validated by and anchored in collaborative conversation and analysis of student work against agreed-upon criteria by teachers across grade levels and subjects?
12. Are report card grades reflective of and illustrated by collections of exemplars and samples that illustrate levels of quality and achievement?

© Adapted from Herbst & Davies (2014) *A Fresh Look at Grading and Reporting in High Schools*, pages 89-90.

SANDRA HERBST

Sandra Herbst is a noted system leader, author, speaker, and consultant with over 20 years of experience in education. Sandra has facilitated professional learning in schools, districts, and organizations across North America and internationally in the areas of leadership, curriculum development, instruction, assessment, and evaluation. She engages her audiences by connecting people to practical and possible strategies and approaches, while building on the expertise and passion that lies within each of us. She was particularly drawn to the field of assessment *for* learning because of the positive results she observed in classrooms, schools, and districts. Sandra is the co-author of the recently published book *A Fresh Look at Grading and Reporting in High Schools* (2014) and is a co-editor of *Quality Assessment in High Schools: Accounts from Teachers* (2013). In 2012, Sandra co-authored the Leaders' Series: *Transforming Schools and Systems Using Assessment: A Practical Guide and Leading the Way to Assessment for Learning: A Practical Guide*. She has several more works in progress in the areas of leadership and assessment.

ANNE DAVIES

As a noted international authority on assessment *for* learning, Dr. Anne Davies's mission is to prepare all learners for their future using assessment *for* learning. Her passion is to support education systems, districts, and schools as they seek to learn and improve using assessment *in the service of* learning. She applies her expert knowledge of developing quality classroom and leadership assessment practices in her continued genuine care and commitment to support educators in the important difference they make every day toward increasing the possibilities of learning for all students. Anne is the author and co-author of more than 30 books and multimedia resources, as well as numerous chapters and articles including the best-seller, *Making Classroom Assessment Work*, now in its third edition, *Leading the Way to Assessment for Learning: A Practical Guide* and recently, with co-author Sandra Herbst, *A Fresh Look at Grading and Reporting in High Schools*.

My Thoughts As I'm Reading

Questions I Have

Ideas to Hang Onto

Resources from connect2learning

The following books and multimedia resources are available from connect2learning.
Discounts are available on bulk orders.

Classroom Assessment Resources

Making Writing Instruction Work .... ISBN 978-1-928092-02-5

Grading, Reporting, and Professional Judgment in Elementary Classrooms ... ISBN 978-1-928092-03-2

Making Classroom Assessment Work – Third Edition .... ISBN 978-0-9867851-2-2

L'évaluation en cours d'apprentissage .... ISBN 978-2-7650-1800-1

A Fresh Look at Grading and Reporting in High Schools .... ISBN 978-0-9867851-6-0

Quality Assessment in High Schools: Accounts From Teachers .... ISBN 978-0-9867851-5-3

Setting and Using Criteria – Second Edition .... ISBN 978-0-9783193-9-7

Établir et utiliser des critères – Deuxième édition .... ISBN 978-0-9867851-7-7

Self-Assessment and Goal Setting – Second Edition .... ISBN 978-0-9867851-0-8

L'autoévaluation et la détermination des objectifs - Deuxième edition .... ISBN 978-0-9867851-9-1

Conferencing and Reporting – Second Edition .... ISBN 978-0-9867851-1-5

Rencontres et communication de l'apprentissage - Deuxième edition .... ISBN 978-1-928092-00-1

Leaders' and Facilitators' Resources

Residency: Powerful Assessment and Professional Practice .... ISBN 978-0-928092-04-9

Lesson Study: Powerful Assessment and Professional Practice .... ISBN 978-0-9867851-8-4

Leading the Way to Assessment for Learning: A Practical Guide .... ISBN 978-0-9867851-3-9

Transforming Schools and Systems Using Assessment:
   A Practical Guide .... ISBN 978-0-9867851-4-6

Protocols for Professional Learning Conversations .... ISBN 978-0-9682160-7-1

When Students Fail to Learn .... ISBN 978-0-9783193-7-3

Assessment for Learning K-12 (Multimedia) .... ISBN 978-0-9783193-8-0

Assessment of Learning: Standards-Based Grading and Reporting
   (Multimedia) .... ISBN 978-0-9736352-8-7

Facilitator's Guide to Classroom Assessment K-12 (Multimedia) .... ISBN 978-0-9736352-0-1

Peace Education

Remember Peace .... ISBN 978-0-9736352-5-6

Seasons of Peace .... ISBN 978-0-9736352-7-0

How To Order

Phone: (800) 603-9888 (toll-free North America)
         (250) 703-2920

Fax: (250) 703-2921

E-mail: books@connect2learning.com

Web: www.connect2learning.com

Post: connect2learning
         2449D Rosewall Crescent
         Courtenay, BC, V9N 8R9
         Canada

---

connect2learning also sponsors events, workshops, and web conferences on assessment and other education-related topics, both for classroom teachers and school and district leaders. Please contact us for a full catalogue.